TRAVELS IN ZANSKAR

ABOUT THE AUTHOR

In his youth Mark Boyden trekked into the Sierra Nevada, Canadian and American Rockies, Pacific Coast Ranges, the Alps and the Himalayas. He is now an Ecologist and Environmental Educator, creator of the StreamScapes Aquatic Education Programme. He lives near Bantry, County Cork with his partner Anneke and four children.

TRAVELS IN ZANSKAR

A JOURNEY TO A CLOSED KINGDOM

MARK BOYDEN

FOREWORD BY DERVLA MURPHY

THE LIFFEY PRESS

Published by
The Liffey Press Ltd
Raheny Shopping Centre, Second Floor
Raheny, Dublin 5, Ireland
www.theliffeypress.com

A catalogue record of this book is
available from the British Library.

ISBN 978-1-908308-51-1

Printed in Ireland by SPRINT-print Ltd

CONTENTS

PREFACE

Many years have passed since my friend and neighbour Paddy O'Hara and I set off to visit the Kingdom of Zanskar. Over the past few winters, I have taken stock of a legacy of photographs, sketches, maps, poems, and copious contemporaneous notes which the expedition had yielded, and have here bound them together, a collection of sincere vignettes, as *Travels in Zanskar*. I have had much encouragement, and wish to thank those patient souls who had hoped to see it sooner. If it seems a bit dated, it is, but I am informed by more recent visitors to Zanskar that this is where the value of the present work lies, as we visited a world and witnessed a culture which has been rapidly and severely eroded since that time.

Come share our journey.

Mark Boyden
October 2013
Bantry, County Cork

Acknowledgements

I wish to acknowledge Peter and Corry Kilroy, Andrew, Chrissy, Sandi, Noel, Mary-Elizabeth and Declan Burke Kennedy – gracious patrons of the expedition.

"Yung-ai !" ("Come in, you are welcome!") – Hopi welcome to Katchina

"...enuma elish..." ("...when on high...") – Akkadian

"We remain caught somewhere between inertia, passion, and light" – Sri Auribindo

FOREWORD

Dervla Murphy

In 1981 the 29-year-old Mark Boyden was privileged to travel
through Zanskar, one of the few Himalayan regions as yet un-
modernised. For political reasons this peripheral province of
old Tibet had remained isolated while elsewhere motor-roads,
and all that those entail, were abruptly ending a way of life that
had survived almost unchanged for millennia. By now the sort
of journey Mark describes, through dramatically beautiful and
hard-to-reach terrain, is no longer possible. Globalisation has
many manifestations. One of them thwarts those of us who en-
joy trekking across landscapes untamed by Western technology – without tunnels through mountains, bridges over chasms,
roads skilfully engineered to diminish the challenge of severe
gradients. In such areas one could, a mere generation ago,
meet peoples who had retained their own cultural integrity –
soon to be damaged by that consumerism which provides our
world's unstable economic foundation.

As we read this book Mark and his companion Paddy
O'Hara and their packhorse "Himself" become our friends.
"Himself" was an essential acquisition. For thousands of

years pack-animals have enabled merchants, scholars and pilgrims to traverse wild territories with which the unaided human physique couldn't cope. Such animals and their owners form a natural team, congenial to and equally dependent on the environment – unlike intrusive 4x4's.

Travels in Zanskar describes an expedition that was not lavishly sponsored and hyped by the media as "daring". It records an old-fashioned journey on a shoe-string, undertaken by two adventurous young men whose preparations, on the practical side were minimal though sensibly adequate. Unlike most present-day travellers, they gladly abandoned all "home comforts" and, while in Zanskar, were content to live as the Zanskaris did. For political reasons no detailed maps were then available, a snag I myself had encountered when trekking through nearby Baltistan in 1975. This however did not deter them; during their expedition they contrived their own map, having taken local advice.

On the intellectual side Mark and Paddy worked hard, before leaving home, to obtain the maximum benefit from their time in this extraordinarily isolated Kingdom. They read widely and studied the relevant Tibetan dialects – that last a considerable feat for people based in the west of Ireland in 1980. Their reward was a rare ability to communicate directly with the Zanskaris; our reward is a travel book in the classic tradition. *Travels in Zanskar* is both a gripping adventure story (every detail rings true) and a sensitive interpretation of an ancient culture on the eve of its demolition. This valuable book reminds us how fast our world is changing, how endangered we are by that speed, and how much has been lost through the imposition of our capitalist ethos on societies from whom we had so much to learn before we destabilised them.

INTRODUCTION

Csoma de Koros, a lifelong wanderer of Hungarian origin, is reputed to have been the first European to visit the Kingdom of Zanskar (literally, Land of Bright Copper) in the course of his expedition of 1826. After this sojourn, there had been very few subsequent visitors from west of the Caucasus up until our expedition of 1981.

A far-flung province of old Tibet, Zanskar's ability to remain culturally intact late into the twentieth century was perhaps due to three chief negative reasons: not being a centre of commerce itself, not being a waypoint on any Silk Route, and perhaps most importantly, the society's seemingly conscious decision to halt technological development, in favour of enhanced spiritual concentration, at some point around 800 years ago (more on this elsewhere).

As India gained independence and prohibited any further internal raj or kingdom in the late 1940s, she then consolidated her claim along the northern trans-Himalayan frontier. With Jammu came Kashmir. With Kashmir came Ladakh. With Ladakh came Zanskar. China, in fulfilling the old emperors' assertion that Tibet is China, occupied Lhasa in the 1950s and, systematically, the remainder of Tibet. The Chinese then proceeded to claim fully a third of Ladakh in the 1962 war with India. The road built by the Indian Army from Srinagar to Leh to mount the defence of Ladakh against this Chinese incursion paved the way for the first significant Indian administrative presence in Ladakh. Zanskar, though functionally the same colour as India on my globe, remained beyond this web, and it was perhaps in response to India's inability to quantify Zanskar that the entire area was, until 1980, placed off limits to visitors. This was why, thus sheltered, Zanskar became the last province of ancient Tibet to retain the old ways intact.

Hence, when word reached us, in 1980, that India had rescinded its ban on travelling to Zanskar (that is, not requiring special licence from Delhi), we began, over winter, to savour the prospect of visiting this venerable old kingdom, and to explore the implications of such a journey. We accepted, at the time, that we would have to prepare for an extremely difficult and arduous expedition which would require us to face extremes of altitude and weather. We also knew that to communicate effectively, and to pursue various multi-disciplinary lines of inquiry, we needed to acquire at least the rudiments of the Tibetan dialogues spoken in those mountains. These matters could be surmounted, but what we had not anticipated was to learn of a considerable obstacle to our plans – as the wider region forms a hub about which radiate Pakistan, Afghanistan, the (now former) USSR, China, India, and Tibet, we were about to walk into a lexicon which included "strategic flashpoint" and "border skirmish". Practically, and on the ground, this meant that detailed maps were not alone unavailable, but even if you could get your hands on one, we then gathered that they were illegal to possess for military intelligence reasons (it will be appreciated that this expedition was undertaken before the advent of either satellite imagery-based topographical maps or Global Positioning Systems).

So over winter we compiled data and drew up our own maps from bits and pieces supplied by either very general, purely indicative, poor quality, or else unreliable charts of the region. For example, a search of *National Geographic* magazine articles revealed that there were two accounts of expeditions into the Indus valley of Ladakh (May 1951 and June 1962) and these had hazily hinted at the geography of adjoining Zanskar. As for the others, from a variety of sources, one mentioned a pass, perhaps an elevation, another denoted a bridge, yet a further denied a village. We collated this data and noted it all into maps which we produced by our own hand. Later, in situ, we were able to further edit and refine these charts through hard-won, on the ground experience, though crudely, on rice paper. Even before setting off, however, we accepted that we would have to rely on dead reckoning, and following our noses.

The other part of the "we" all of this refers to was a special partner and collaborator. I had previously been associated, in work and pleasure, with my neighbour Paddy O'Hara. There is something foreboding about Paddy until you get within range of the glint in his eye. Tall, strapping, full sable-bearded, ascetic, deliberate, resourceful, a superb craftsman and original thinker. Sharing an interest in Zanskar, we together hatched a plan and determined a journey. Paddy would call of a winter's evening and, as the curlews' call heralded fresh rain blowing in from the Atlantic, we would sit around the glowing fire and share our research. Given that the sources were scanty, we nonetheless pooled what we could find, and in the spring we headed off. On a lark, and in the spirit of the occasion, we took assumed names for the travels, which reflected our oriental literary tastes. He became "Li Tai Po" (after the Taoist poet), and I adopted "Kai Lung", Ernest Bramah's wandering story-teller from Chinese antiquity, whose name some translate as "Outside Dragon", though the more sardonic prefer to see it rendered as "Hot Air".

Our ramblings curiously mirrored those of a pair of fellow celestial travellers. One or two may allow that Saturn was the condition that year (my twenty-ninth), and Jupiter the opportunity, as they were hand-in-hand, in extraordinary conjunction, even in retrograde, for nine months and more, and this marked the true time of my tale. Throughout the expedition they hung there nightly in glistening splendour, their doubled twinkling beams both guiding and witnessing this venture, before they too parted, and wandered their own ways once more.

With impeccable timing, my dizzy marriage dissolved just at this time, but somehow even this could not dissuade my intent but, in the circumstance, redoubled my resolve to ascend to lofty bedrock, if for no other reason than to gain perspective. In early April I had my kit and rucksack assembled. With deep feeling I bid farewell to my children. Then J. called and I climbed into his Morris, and he took me over the Priest's Leap Road into County Kerry, and I did not look back. The following is a collection of moments from those travels, together with an effort to relate some reliable documentary information upon life in Zanskar.

❁   ❁

A story for that lover of stories, Anneke; and for my children, Rhea, Tadhg, Owen, and Amelia, and my intrepid fellow traveller, Paddy O'Hara

Field Map of Zanskar Region

1.

OUR DESCENT THROUGH THE CENTURIES

We flew from Paris to Delhi, and this act commenced our descent through the centuries. Under dense predawn darkness we made our way down from the airport into the old city, down into yesterday's suspended myrrh and coriander, charcoal and paraffin, jasmine and dung, which competed, compressed and homogenised with an evaporated sea of urine to produce the city's unique ambience – with me craving mountain air! Morning broke with a clamour and, after finding lodgings, by noon we learned that on the next day, or the next, an overnight train would take us to Jammu, four hundred odd miles north. From Jammu, a two-day bus ride would see us over the Pirpanjal Mountains to Kashmir. Up the Himalayan slopes, on the eastern border of Kashmir, lies Zoji-la, the one viable mountain pass leading to Ladakh, and Ladakh, in turn, offered the portal through the Zanskar Mountains to reach the Kingdom.

Mid-April, strictly speaking, was too early to be trekking, but the plan was to advance quickly to Kashmir and, from this base, watch the weather and be poised to persevere east at the first seasonal opportunity. The hope was to be over the Himalayas as the snows eased, southeast from Kargil into Zanskar for some months, and back out due south over the Himalayas into the Himachal Pradesh before the snows packed back on again with Autumn.

So I gave three days to Delhi, though all I have is a shorthand paragraph for this consummate distraction as I had not sought this, only to gain the snows and ascend into a new world. But resourcefulness is everything, and within hours I had thrown myself into this sprawling chaos. Without focus or intent I ranged out along the bright avenues of the new city, or digressed down the dark sweaty markets of the old, always with the compelling heat and weighted air. The greatest moments of grace involved meetings with those preparing the glorious food, the making of which had been handed down the millennia with absolute sensibility. Sated but perplexed, I would return through the hot dead April nights to the relative tranquillity of our chambers at the hostelry.

On the final evening I wandered in to find Paddy sorting countless small-denomination rupee notes (which, we had been informed, would be handy in the mountains) on his bed by candlelight when the ceiling fan, celebrating the end of a power outage, burst into life, scattering his lucre about the room. A brass and bagpipe band erupted in the street and, drawn to the balcony by this cacophony, I watched a wedding march pass by, featuring a shy groom astride an albino elephant. When all of this mirth had finally eased I lay my reeling head down. Restless as strychnine, drifting between waking and sleeping, I entered a phantasm in which there was much importance and tension attached to finding a mirror. When I could not locate one anywhere, comfort and resolution came, as might only in a dream, with a decision to head north.

Hence it was, upon the following night, that I awoke, gladly, and considerably further north, on the Delhi–Jammu "express", disturbed by the silence of the halted train. Across the rail lines, an enormous black locomotive was shimmering in a night siding with a seemingly needless head of steam up as, alongside, a pyjama-clad boy attendant was pouring tea for the Sikh driver and fireman who were bent over their Parcheesi on an upturned crate beside the rails, the whole scene lit by their gas lamp. The fireman raised his teacup to his lips as we moved off with a metallic jolt, and I returned to further dream. Dawn roused me, again to the halted train, but this time in a station whose name I'll never know, peopled by a crowd of swaying colours.

As it was breakfast time, passing vendors were hailed and scalding tumblers of tea, nan breads, and rupee coins were exchanged through the barred open windows of our carriage. Just at midday the train clattered and swayed into Jammu, the summer capital of all that India and Pakistan have continued to contest since their respective liberations from the Raj. Being a scant few miles across the northern plain from the mutually resented frontier, we arrived into the midst of ostentatious displays of martial readiness. Mindless adolescent soldiers paraded about in heavily-armed abandon against a background of throaty roars issued by convoys of countless tanks, while MIG fighters tore the sky to shreds overhead.

Prior to being deposited into this ghastly scene, we had half-wondered if we might pass a day and a night here, but the palpable and repugnant smell of war contrasted so vehemently with our first glimpse of misty foothills to the northeast of the dusty city that we decided to immediately locate a Kashmir-bound bus.

Receiving directions to the departure point, we were delayed further only by the solicitations of a freelance ear-cleaner. An array of pig-iron instruments, generally variations on corkscrews, hung off a large key ring about his waist. He and members of his guild might, without warning, slip one of these implements half-way inside your head and, in withdrawing it, produce a stone, or an insect, or a cat's eye, or a simple ball of wax and hair. Having displayed the enticing sample, for a fee he would be happy to complete the task. But having parried the initial thrust Paddy and I both insisted that our ears were clean and, regretfully, not in need of his ministrations. As we withdrew I looked back and saw him longingly eyeing our ears.

Locating our Baltistani bus, we skipped up its steps and exchanged bows with its driver. As we chose our seats, we remarked with surprise at how empty the bus seemed. This observation was instantly countered, as no sooner had it been uttered than we were then joined and squeezed-up by a bevy of flightless birds, seven young lambs, two calves, a most incongruous array of scrap metal lashed to a pallet, and endless bundles of swag all borne aboard by a crew of wondrous fellow humans in animate chatter. With departure time seemingly determined by the bus being stuffed to the gunwales, its beleaguered starter motor finally engaged in a fetching "oh-no-oh-no-oh-no-oh-no-here-we-go-again-brrrooom", and the driver, with two clenched fists and considerable effort, persuaded the gear-stick into first.

Leaving the dusty accidental war behind, we climbed the while into welcome coniferous mists, the remainder of the day winding around mountain roads while the yelps, whoops and cries of those aboard ceased only when, for equilibrium, all necks (even the birds') would studiously crook into the cornering of a given tight bend. As night fell the journey broke in the village of Batoté, and we were told to rejoin the bus at eight in the morning to continue. A small group of people had met the bus to offer passengers food and lodging for the night and, for an agreeable fee, we followed our favourite solicitor home to his sprawling and spirited family. This was now the heart of *garam masala* country, and to the mutton and potatoes they added seriously pungent leeks and onions which they were able to keep in the ground through the winter, all of it served with an innate grace. As no common tongue arose between our English and their Urdu, we found hilarious resort in sign language, before discourse effortlessly turned to song. They sang melodic rondos and laments; we responded with broken-heart ballads.

Encountering absolute hospitality must be considered one of the Wonders of the World. Like love, it is always the same, and always infinitely varied. One's every need of food and drink, of silence and communion, that elusive sense of feeling-at-home, all appearing without effort. Wherever it is met in the world, the unanticipated sense of welcome is the most magnificent balm to the weary traveller, invariably coloured by the *esprit loci*. Here we met a Muslim hue, which tonight combined satiation and jovial society with a solemn duty of care.

Hence, as we rose to depart to our dormitory cabin under the rain forest firs, our host commenced an unexpected mime. "This is," he uttered by forming guns with his hands, kicking an imaginary door down with his foot, effecting furtive movements with his eyes, and jerking his thumb in the direction of the uncle of the house, "serious bandit country, so my brother here will sleep outside your door to protect you for the night."

"This is not intended to put you off your sleep, so good-night," he concluded, by leaning his head into twinned hands, smiling deeply through closed eyes and feigning a snore. When he would not heed our objections, Paddy and I thanked them with bows and retired to our bunks, where we drifted off composing and reciting snippets extempore. Here's one:

Saturated with Delhi
we rose up out of the plain
hot curry on my belly
but here there's been cool rain

❋ ❋

2.

THE CLEMENT VALE

As we stepped out in the morning, we tucked a gratuity under the woollen blanket covering the now-sleeping brother outside our door, and skipped on down the forested road to find our beloved Kashmir-bound bus. Its rumbling idle suggested that it was now raring to go and, before long, we were all leaning once more like cyclists into the bends to help the coach corner, resuming our climb through the robust Himalayan pines and cedars. Evermore steeply it rose, but for only another hour when we gained the Banihal Tunnel at the summit of the Pirpanjal Mountain range.

Being *the* land-link for India's assertion of sovereignty in Kashmir (and for some, a detested umbilical), this road had become a strategic avenue, with its weak point at the tunnel being flanked by cannon and no-nonsense. With large signs demanding "No Photographs" in eight languages, only the birds remained cackling, though now with somewhat muted misgiving, as weapon-waving men made their way slowly down the aisle, not yielding to our proposed transit of *their* tunnel until they had gazed, Medusa-like, into all our eyes and, haughtily satisfied that there were no saboteurs in our midst, withdrawn once more.

From here it could only be downhill all the way. The ebul-
lience returned to what had now become a distinct culture riding the bus. We rode, as upon a river, down tumbling cascades
and frenzied riffles into the well-eddied meanders of the fertile
Kashmir vale before being deposited, as so much silt, into the
city.

Upon our arrival in Srinagar we promptly sought out further water, though now less allegorical, or were perhaps
pushed there by the unwanted urban assault we encountered
on the streets. From a wide choice of lodgings proffered by the
throng who greeted us, we agreed to rent a houseboat from a
Mr. Farrouz and his family who lived in another boat lashed
together with twenty more to form one of hundreds of some
such "neighbourhoods" on Dal Lak, an azure body of water
astride the Kashmiri capital.

Above us, our host informed us as he paddled us to our new
abode, four feet of snow remained on Zoji-la, with frequent
storms, though we thought, perhaps shamefully, that these
observations may have been in the interests of securing our
long-term tenancy. But we unpacked and set up housekeeping
as if we might be there awhile, then conferred on deck as the
hot sun split the deodar shingles on the shallow-pitched roof of
the cabin. We could see the heavily laden snowy mountains to
the east, and knew that we would have to wait, perhaps a few
weeks or more, before venturing towards the pass to Ladakh.
So be it, for preparatory chores remained to be dealt with. It
would take some time to finalise our provisions and gear for
the expedition ahead.

The clement vale offered the last opportunity to acquire
walnuts, rice, almonds, lemons, garlic – we wished to carry ra-
tions sufficient for a few months, as in Ladakh and Zanskar our

queries had revealed that we would otherwise have access to only barley, wheat, butter and peas.

Further, Paddy and I had put off the decision as to whether or no to acquire an animal (or two) to share the trek, but amongst our many and necessary deliberations, we now considered the companionship of at least a donkey, or an agreeable yak, which would enable us not only to share the burden of provisions, but also provide additional company in landscapes which we had come to believe would be devoid of other diversion. And indeed, a four-legged partner might provide very useful introduction to, or at least common ground for discussion with, those who we would travel amongst. As an afterthought, Paddy emerged from one of his contemplative reveries to poignantly remind me that Genghis Khan had made the mistake of bringing animals from lower countries into higher ones, with the consequence that all had perished due to their inadaptability to extreme altitude. The lesson being that, when travelling to high country, avoid acquiring a beast until you get there.

The valley's days were mostly calm, warming, with a quickening of spring bird activity, though storms passed like dirty grey waves across the formidable Himalayas to the east, and we knew Zoji-La was no place to be just yet. Hours were passed with each going off in his own direction, or just remaining aboard our houseboat, the gently rocking ambience a wonderful backdrop for studying, sunning or dozing off.

As all outings began and ended by water, these journeys were effected by the *shikara* which had been placed at our disposal. *Shikara* are wonderful craft, essentially light-weight canoes, flared at bow and stern, which sit high in the water, propelled effortlessly by a single J-stroked paddle from the stern, and they invited use. Dal Lak has wonderful expanses, interrupted by (man-made?) islands and causeways, all worthy of sublimely stroked exploration. When visiting the city, one could tie one's *shikara* up along a quay wall and know that, abandoned, its security was sacrosanct.

On these latter urban outings there may at times be a mission; upon others I sought only an aimless ramble through the markets. As an outsider in Kashmir, one is constantly targeted and badgered to purchase any and all. The competition is intense, with promises of undying friendship attending entreaties to buy goods. Though this can be wearisome, one also meets plenty of kindness and sincerity, and I found something I liked in most I met.

The last thing I might have needed was an oversized carpet (however attractive), but it struck me upon one of my purposeless rambles through the extensive commercial sector, how can one justify an indifferent neutrality in the marketplace? If I wasn't going to buy, then surely I must have something to sell? Pondering this predicament while I rounded a corner into the cloth quarter, I spotted the father of an enterprise setting his two sons to pounce upon me, and in an instant they had conducted me, irresistibly, into the family stall. Bolts and loose ends of bright cottons, stunning tweeds, and muted cashmeres were hove-to in piles. Each of the three of them caught up one or another pattern and weave and, in turn, drew my attention. They were excellent salesmen, but it just wasn't going to work upon someone who was going to have to carry all possessions upon his back.

Finally, the father asked, "How do they sell cloth where you come from? How would you lay out our stall?"

I didn't say more than, "Well, em...", before they were suddenly convinced that I could revolutionise their business! So I had something to sell (in Kashmir!), and without further delay I walked back out into the street to survey their pitch.

After a bit of thought, I pronounced, "If you had display racks, maybe intersecting here, leaving a central space to unfurl your sample, hmm, yes, full bolts horizontal on thick doweling, with about a foot of tail to catch the eye, loose ends and bargains in this quarter, in the view of passers-by...". Though dusk was near, carpenters were summonsed immediately, and, hammer-and-tongs, A.K. and his sons had a new shop before midnight!

A carpetbagger along the Way
chanced upon a vagabond;
Queried he, "now does it pay
to simply let the world go round?"

The vagabond to this replied,
"I can't allay compassion,"
The busy man, he fairly cried,
"You're only fit for lashin'"

The vague one said,
"You surely see the mutual intrusion;
I did not ask for charity,
just empathy for illusion."

❋   ❋

With word of heavy snow in the mountains, we saw that we would have at least a second week in Kashmir. To vary our stay we moved out of our Dal Lak houseboat to a new abode, another bright and cheery boat but over on the other side of Srinagar, lashed to the bank of the River Jellum. Parsimonious Paddy was happy – it was a rupee a day cheaper – and now Ali Guna and his family became our equally amenable hosts.

As on the lake, a *shikara*, piloted by a paddling aquatic shopkeeper and loaded to the gunwales as a cornucopia with fruit, fresh cut cornflowers and roses, spring greens, cotton bags of flour and a hundred spices, glided between houseboats supplying needs. Daily we hailed him for our breakfast supplies, and flowers to arrange in our cabins. Manoeuvring his boat, he would commence reciting the contents of his current store in lowly sonorous tones as he approached across the becalmed shore side waters. Where is he now with his languid idyll?

Apart from dining out occasionally in the city, we generally took our main evening rice with the family. This was pure theatre, dedicated to the art of ergonomics and minimal effort to achieve a great deal, here and now a superb meal. In preparation and cooking, the patriarch had organised himself so that he never needed to move from his seat on the floor before the low clay stove. His chopping board set before him, his spices in various containers on his right, his fuel in a vessel to his left, rolling out and firing flatbreads, frying meats and vegetables over the charcoal fire, issuing instructions to or counselling his children the while. Afterwards, as the family dispersed and the three of us were left alone, he would pull his hobble-bobble near as we wound down the day.

Maps continued to be a source of concern. In Zanskar we were headed into an unforgiving and desolate wilderness where errors would not be tolerated. So we were happy beyond measure when Paddy returned from a visit to the used-book and-document quarter of the market with another scrap for our collection. Though short on variation from what we already possessed, the evening was nonetheless given over to its gleaning, and it yielded a few more pieces of precious information for our map-in-progress.

From our new vantage I watched the River Jellum morning, noon, and night as its flow revealed the weather above us at ten to twenty thousand feet. When early May radiance put the Himalayan snows melting, the Jellum rose throughout the day. Locals said it was too early to travel into the mountains, advising us to wait *another month* even unto June. This was a claustrophobic prospect for me; I was ever eager to get to Zoji-la. Once we passed beyond that portal, however, we would be beyond postal service for some months and therefore completely out of touch. As I wanted to receive the last possible word that all was well back home, I acquiesced and rented a bicycle. A day's cycle took me out around Dal Lak to the Moguls' Shalimar gardens, where, given the vale's setting, paradise had been restored. Back across the ambitious causeway the lake was alive with bird life! Brilliant turquoise and orange kingfishers piercing the lake's surface to feed; a multitude of oversized kites never on a course but always changing their flight's intent, darkening the sky with their span; and raucous heronries in the poplar tops, not unlike the markets.

3.

ZOJI-LA

To dispose of his final business, Paddy would remain in Kashmir for another week. But I, unable to resist the heights any longer (and having had a telegram from Declan in Dublin saying all was well back home), caught a predawn bus which was heading east up out of the lower vale. The better part of the day saw no more than fifty miles ground out, the road being clear of snow as far as the alpine-like village of Sonamarg. Here the bus could go no further, so the remaining daylight was spent hiking into the lowest snows to a point part way up the Zoji-la where I found lee from the wind and encamped for the night.

I hoped to start the following morning with first light and make it over the pass, but awoke to a blizzard which drove me back down into the valley, and I sought shelter at the small army post at Baltal. There I met a fellow backpacker who was trying to reach Leh (the capital of Ladakh), and we agreed to cross the pass together on the next clear day. We chatted as we spread out our gear and set up housekeeping in a small clean cabin to which the soldiers had kindly assigned us. He was competent and literate, so I welcomed the idea of having his company for the transit of Zoji-la. But an hour later, while

14

just outside our hut, he surprised the camp's dogs and they savaged him. Only stones and shouts from their masters and myself managed to finally distract them, as they had bitten his legs badly and, in complete frenzy, had him on the ground. A driver was readied to take him back to Srinagar for treatment and rabies vaccination. He was in a lot of pain, but even as the jeep pulled away, he vowed to make Leh yet, and I believed he would.

Satisfied that the dogs were secured, I went for an afternoon walk a ways up the route to the Amarnath shrine, an important Hindi pilgrimage in season. I wandered until the path was blocked by a fresh avalanche of snow (yet even this a good sign of spring). A gloriously intense sun broke through, and I paused beside a stream which was starting to sing with the thaw. Where a man toils or rests, surely a robin shall appear, and indeed her curiously tiny Himalayan cousin flew from a lone birch to land at my feet and see what my disturbance had turned up.

When I looked out of my cabin before sunrise the few bright stars still remaining suggested a cloudless and promising morning. Having been assured that the camp's dogs would be housed for the night, I jumped into my corduroys, pulled on my top layers, laced up my boots and, shouldering my burden, headed out to cross the silver valley back to the road. I had made two hundred yards from the camp when I heard the barks and yelps erupt behind me. The full pack was thundering towards me and I knew there was no escape from these mastiffs. In haste, I whipped off my rucksack and unsheathed my knife, filled with panic and dread as to what I might do. In a moment the lead dog attacked, but as he made his leap for me, I jumped in the air and as with a volley kicked him as hard

15

as I could with my heavy boot. This broke not only his jaw and several of his teeth, for he flailed wailing upon his side, but as importantly the resolve of the pack, which then kept their distance. Now the soldiers appeared from the camp, calling their dogs back, but half-heartedly, and the insane thought entered my mind that this, perhaps, was sport to them. I knew that with the perennial threat of war and a siege mentality they valued their canine defence, but, full of adrenaline, I was less than elegant with my hosts, cursing at some volume their dogs, their cause, and any thoughts they may hold in their fecking heads. I warily regarded the other dogs, now cowed, as I regathered my rucksack and headed out across the valley floor. They tended to their broken dog and I feared, as I strode away, that they may put a bullet in my back.

Gaining the road again, I rose and, as the dry snow underfoot squeaked and deepened, I moved into pine woods and considered my fate. I perceive that my emotional process is reasonably expeditious – if I experience a feeling of fair to middling intensity, I express it and move on. The greater passions are left for me to ponder, like lost love which I would examine exhaustively from every side for some time to come. And now, in anger and confusion, with a dog most likely dead and horrendous insults hurled at fellow humans, I was condemned to consider and revisit all that had transpired that morning with every step of the ascent of Zoji-la. But do steps not eventually bring peace to every predicament?

By the time I reached the summit before noon, my act of self-preservation had reassumed preeminence. I had secured a peace of sorts, and my focus returned to the way before me. Midday clouds once more prevailed, and the temperature plummeted, so I hastened along, hoping to drop into a valley, but the Zoji-la is a drawn-out pass which levels off along a ridge for some miles. In the midst of this greying bleakness I noticed snow leopard's prints aimlessly criss-crossed by those of a barefoot human's. The way opened, and I spotted the author of the human prints, a speck of a man across the snow-field. He became aware of me, and changed his direction so that within twenty minutes we came face to face.

He was an elderly *Sadhu* (Hindi holy man), clad only in a ragged trailing cotton garment more suitable to the clement elements of Tamil Nadu. Planting his staff in the snow, we exchanged "*Namaste*" as we were both compelled to stare at each other at some length, and he was an extraordinary man to gaze upon. Though he did not shiver, in every sense his wide eyes and weathered countenance proclaimed over-exposure. Strangely, his expression ranged widely. One moment he was eminently serene, then, and this was astounding, as it was achieved without moving a single facial muscle, his look expressed abject horror, which as easily became reverential awe or spiteful mocking. I had some walnuts handy, so I retrieved them from a pocket and offered them to him. After we exchanged bows, our gazes averted to our destinations and we each went our way.

An hour later, as I began to descend, I met a feral yak – a big, shaggy black yak, which bolted before I got within a hundred yards of it. But this meant that I was in Ladakh, and it was all the welcome I had hoped for. I felt that Zoji-la must be one of those places in the world where the wind begins, and indeed as I progressed through that day it scored me as if it was fresh off the whetstone. Whereas the west side of the pass had featured groves of birch and the Asian pines, their lush carpets of mulch amidst the snows which in season I imagined sustaining wild grasses and flowers, the east side was barren of trees, with a stony underlay. It was with much joy and relief then that, after dropping sharply through this harsh landscape for a few hours, I came upon a patch of royal blue iris flowering, against all of these cold grey odds, where a spring arose in the shelter of some raised bedrock which held what sun might shine. In the presence of such beauty need and want coalesced, and I was now allowed to face what I had denied myself for so many miles and hours against this unforgiving wind – a desire to gather my scattered self and access some overdue relief within sheltered and agreeable surrounds. Here I halted and ate more walnuts flavoured with half an onion. Then, on a suitable contour in the hard earth, I rolled out my little rug to keep me from the cold when reclining, and dozed off counting mountains and dogs.

Suddenly I was under arrest. The day had begun with soldiers and was destined to end with soldiers. After bidding farewell to the irises I had reassumed my burden, took not forty steps and, dropping out of this comely escarpment, saw the patrol as they saw me. "With bears and armed men never change your pace" so, smiling, I walked straight up to them and, thankfully taking me to be a pilgrim, they lowered their lethal Enfield .303's and escorted me back to their base, where I was to await an interview with the officer in charge. The arrest was propitious; wanting to travel light, I had left the tent with Paddy in Kashmir. I was otherwise going to have to keep an eye out for a cave or some cradling overhang to shelter from what had the makings of a nasty night.

At their camp, their Lieutenant and I discussed my route, destination, purpose, and then branched off into current world affairs, the shocking price of turmeric, and the amount of time which had passed since we had last seen our families. This was all by way of his assessing my character and reliability. Satisfied that I was harmless, he nevertheless issued a stern warning that a rival Pakistani patrol may not view me so sympathetically. He did not insist upon searching me, but I was glad that all of my mapping resources were stealthily stitched into my backpack lining. He assigned the best English-speaker among the men to shadow me, the chief concern being to escort me through the field of landmines outside the Nissen (or Quonset) hut when I must relieve myself.

With the day that was in it I found myself preferring mines to dogs, which they did not possess (as they are mutually exclusive), though I did not discuss my experience at Baltal. Things loosened up after dark. It turned out I was the first outside soul they'd seen all winter. The Lieutenant broke out some rum, and the cook brought me tinned curried mutton and army-issue *papadams*. A boy of a soldier shared his melodious soprano with us, plaintively intoning a Hindi love song. I offered Dylan's "If Today Was Not an Endless Highway", with feeling.

Promptly at 7:30 the stove was stoked up for the night and the paraffin lamps quenched. As I drew my sleeping bag up in the dark, outside the frozen gale howled around and racked the tin hut. While twenty soldiers snored around me, I dreamt that it seemed like so many first steppes – the Hindi lowland, the Sikh north plain, and Kashmir the Prophet's. Then the yak had welcomed me to the Buddhist landscape.

In the morning they fired up their half-track vehicle and gave me a ride for a few miles downstream as a guise for a patrol. Wishing me *Namaste* as farewell, they wheeled around and headed back west, while I wandered east into a crisp clear-skied morning, descending into the Dras River valley. Barren, near-vertical canyon walls kept me in cold shadow until at midday, in an expanse of the valley floor, I got my first view of the village of Matayan. From a distance its assertive mosque offered a beacon of hope for the lonely traveller.

As the denizens here, too, had not met anyone from the west over winter, women and men broke from domestic and farming chores to circle about and welcome me as I entered the streets. They were tough and beautiful. The women wore enormous silver earrings and smiles. As the men gathered, they easily slipped their arms affectionately around each other as they viewed their visitor. Here, where there was a smattering of English, they asked me, "And what is your sweet name?"

They appeared to argue (thankfully, in a positive sense) as to which house would receive me with hospitality, but eventually it was agreed upon, and most adjourned from their tasks to come watch me drink sweet tea and consume a very welcome spicy goat and whole barley stew. I had no sooner finished this, though, when conversation halted abruptly as word came through that the daily Kargil-bound lorry was about to leave the village and would I accept the offer of a lift to help me on my way east? A hasty leave-taking was less than seemly in the midst of such a welcome but, being without vehicles themselves and knowing full well how this lorry would further my journey, they elegantly walked me down to the departure point and waved me out with great vigour and blessing.

From here the road was clear of snow, and as we lumbered along, the fluent English-speaking driver and I became fast friends over common concerns. With dread he referred me to sites along the road which had been the scene of disgraceful carnage in the most recent Indian–Pakistani "skirmishes". His mood picked up when discussing his family. As we dropped with the river, there were more frequent patches of verdure, and the season advanced by the mile. Where the River Dras met the River Shingo, I begged the driver to allow me to walk the remaining miles to Kargil, which he did so reluctantly.

Rambling downstream, the landscape became positively lush in comparison with what I had traversed since Kashmir. This was largely due to the efforts of local farmers, whose plantations of apricot trees crowded the far banks, and here and there wheat and barley were well sprouted. Around another bend, four children looked up from their game and ran to me, uttering their only English, "Candy, candy". I wasn't carrying sweets, but I did have a few spare pencils, which I broke in half and sharpened with my knife. Tearing up a few sheets of precious paper, they became so absorbed in line and design that they took no notice of my leaving.

4.

THE BAZAAR OF KARGIL

The bazaar of Kargil clusters about the confluence of the Rivers Dras, Shingo and Suru. After assuming the latter's name they together flow northwest to contribute a substantial tributary to the Indus. The town's main *raison d'etre* is its being on this, one of the old routes between Persia and China, as well as a crossroads for the road north to Skardu and, to a lesser extent, southeast into the Zanskar region. The resultant population, those who through the centuries have said, "We'll stay here," are a fantastic mix of skin colour, bone structure, costume and religious vision, which I observed as, with dusk closing, I walked the streets critically eyeing various hostelries before entering under the attractive and gaily-painted sign of the Yak Tail Hotel.

The proprietor prepared a meal of rice and beans and ate with me. He told me I was the first outsider to reach Kargil this year, and hoped I would be patient with all of the queries I would receive about news from the outside. Bearing a taper he led me to a cold deserted dormitory, and seated himself, still regaling, on one bed as I undressed and wearily sought my sleeping bag upon another. He knew *everything*, but my eyelids failed and his voice melted like snow and filled the river which flowed past the apricot trees, past the monument which marked the place where Lieutenant R. had been killed by a shell burst, became children's laughter and then compressed into absolute darkness.

I spent a few days judging my ground, garnering some geography here, picking up a Tibetan phrase there, seeking several disinterested estimates on the price of local horses, and generally exploring Kargil and its immediate hinterland. Returning from a walk along the north bank of the Suru one evening, I was perplexed to see the resident Tibetan Buddhists scurrying along various backstreets, seemingly in response to the muezzin's call to prayers. Then a full May moon rose over the bleak and still wintry eastern landscape, and I realised that it was the lunar phase (indeed, the Buddha's Birth, Death and Enlightenment Day) which the Buddhists were gathering to commemorate, at the same hour in which the Muslims were seeking their Mosque.

My queries about the local ponies, and what one may expect to pay, led me to Habib Ullah, agricultural advisor to the western Ladakh region. Habib is from Kashmir, educated in Delhi, and we enjoyed each other's company so much at first meeting that we then met regularly at a tea shop perched out over the Suru. I was intensely interested in recent developments in agriculture, including new strands of salix willow and poplar being planted as short-rotation and coppiced timber. Habib told me of the organisation of local apricot growers into a co-operative marketing structure. And he was full of tips about the venture which awaited us to the southeast in Zanskar. As to horses, we must decide if we wish to have a *kulay* (slow) or *jhokspa* (fast) one, as the horses are bred for different paces as well as various loads and altitudes.

Electricity supply for Kargil is provided by a diesel-powered unit, which comes on at sunset for three hours, after which the town goes to bed. Though the cold moon now waned and rose ever later, the intense crystal firmament lit the frosted empty streets sufficiently to allow a walk through the hushed market. A facade, which might be bustled past in daytime, became curious by starlight. The stalls stood silent, but here I could now shed my mild agoraphobia and find the peace to pause and ponder the echoes of the daylight hubbub. Even the Suru had been silenced, and by night had become a tamely shimmering silver ribbon. Circling and turning and feeling the chill, I headed back to the Yak Tail and, feeling my way up through the pitch of the stairway, found my room and bed and, lighting a candle, reached for my pen.

> *Kargil. Beneath the stars, circled*
> *by peaks, rim of faint white*
> *somehow ringing.*
>
> *In the sleeping town, not a sound*
> *save a child of the night*
> *lies teething.*
>
> *May moon saw, mongoloids in velvet*
> *celebrate the Buddha.*
> *Who taught the River Suru has no past,*
> *the Suru has no future.*

❄   ❄

In the morning I wandered back down a little lane which I had discovered during the night. Now it was a hive of industry, mostly tradesmen's premises, where a variety of smiths were persuading matter to assume desirable shapes and functions, while young apprentices steadied the other end. My destination was a workshop where I had noticed, upon the previous night's stroll, some squared timber leaning against a gable, and sure enough there was the carpenter at work assembling one of those pleasing window frames with rounded corners which one associates with Tibetan houses. To my delight, his English was such that we were able to discuss the merits and employment of the locally available timbers, hard and soft. And now, in the light of day, I was able to inspect them.

The walnut and apricot were dense, heavy, and beautifully grained, and, though available only in short thick scantlings, were turned for bowls, chopping boards and rolling pins. The willows and poplar, which I had noticed growing in abundance, were softer and more quickly grown, but with beautiful figure and worthy of Brian Boru's harp. With pride the craftsman displayed his ingenious tools, all self-made, and when he saw me linger over a beautiful apricot-bodied plane, he offered it to me. His apprentice crouched beside us the while, slack-jawed, hanging on our conversation.

I hastened to make my rendezvous for afternoon tea with Habib Ullah to advance my tutorial upon all things agrarian. When we had drained our cups, he returned to his many tasks but I, without further current ambition, sought out my loft for a nap, and slept until I was awakened by footsteps on the stairs and my landlord's voice addressing a customer: "Kind sir, the only other room I have to offer, I'm afraid you will have to share," when the door opened and in he stepped, with Paddy in tow! The Zoji-la had been ploughed of snow, Paddy had come over on one of the season's first lorries, randomly chosen

"When he saw me linger over a beautiful apricot-bodied plane, he offered it to me."

the same guesthouse which I had fallen upon, and had just received the same tour of the Yak Tail which I had upon arrival!

United again, we set to in earnest finalising our travel plans. We pooled information and took decisions on questions of travel, diet and the extent of the kit we would carry. Evenings we would repair to Ravi Singh's restaurant for one of his incomparable Balti curries, sharing tables with other clientele who consisted of local teachers, civil servants and the occasional soldier. There was much to be learned of day-to-day goings on, and we ourselves were cross-examined by those who, starved for outside company by the winter, wanted to know more about what was developing in the world. Through India and Kashmir, and right up here into western Ladakh, Ireland was well known (fellow former colony). Every aspect of Irish life was queried, though the biggest wonder was generated by photos we showed of the hedge-rowed, patchwork fields back home, and how did the grass remain green year round without irrigation? Indeed!

An early round of the Bazaar saw us acquire a primus stove together with a gallon of paraffin oil, so as to lessen our impact upon what Habib had impressed upon me would be scarce indigenous fuel supplies (twigs and dung) for our cooking needs in the mountains. Having decided to buy a horse, I sought the merchants out a further time, now seeking a bolt-end of burlap, together with a large needle and appropriate thread to enable me to make saddlebags.

I joined a group of people pressing up against a general merchandise stall, where the proprietor sat cross-legged on a platform at about shoulder level, open to the street, and within arm's reach about him produced a variety of hardware as it was demanded. There seemed to be no end to his inventory, yet still he had not moved from his squat. I was nearing the front, confident of miming my needs when, behind me, there was a stir, and the crowd parted to allow a ragged and intense looking ascetic to approach.

Placing a few rupee coins on the platform, he muttered his requirement, and the merchant, with an expression of "no trouble at all", reached into one of his chests of drawers, produced a vial, and from it measured out a quantity of quicksilver on his finest scales. This he parcelled for the ascetic, who then spun on his heel and, doubtlessly, returned to his alchemy. I acquired my sewing needs and, returning to the Yak Tail, passed the remainder of the morning stitching away until I had fashioned my saddlebags. When it was completed, I held it aloft to judge, and began to get curious as for whom I had tailored it.

In the afternoon I would again be meeting Habib for tea, so I asked Paddy to join us as I knew he would savour the scene. We found Habib there before us, sitting on that unlikely balcony cantilevered out over a now raging and churned up River Suru. For Paddy's benefit we dredged back through previous discussions, talking horses, prices, feeding requirements at high altitude, shoeing, health and all matters of equestrian well-being. Paddy enjoyed the agrarian conversation, and warmed up even more when the conversation turned to cattle (ever the O'Hara, ever the Corkman!). Habib glowed when I related that I had sold a Kerry cow and calf at the April Fair on Bantry Square to finance the current expedition, and then agreed (to our delight) to relate the Genealogy of the Yak, which I reproduce for you on the following page.

Habib went back to his work. Paddy and I strolled across the suspension bridge to the north bank where established willows of some considerable girth grew along the Suru channel. Coppiced poplars extended back from these riverside trees as hedges, and in their shelter the wheat was already long enough to wave a bit in the breeze. We moved on through flowering apricot groves when, through the boughs, we glimpsed a mosque under construction and were compelled to take a closer look. Only the heavy timber principles had been raised so far, but these gracefully adzed arches tenoned into considerable mortised posts hinted at the beauty and substance of what was being built. We were agog at the presence of such timeless joinery, lowering our wandering gazes to acknowledge the inspiration and devotion of the artisans who were founding them.

We were ready to depart Kargil. The winter receded, and our provisions and gear were now fully assembled. I passed a last afternoon in the District wandering upstream along a small tributary which I had noticed descended steeply from

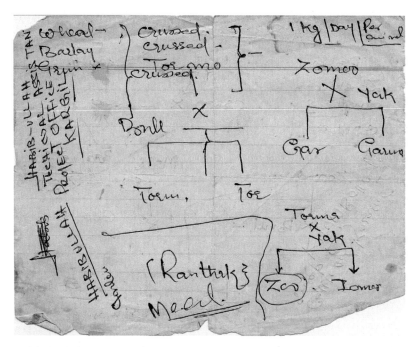

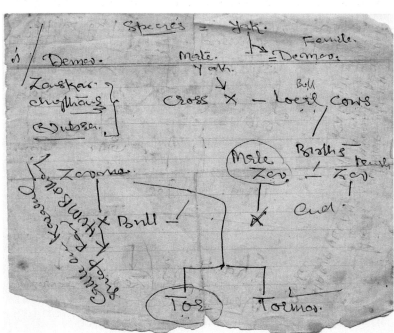

"The Genealogy of the Yak" – from Habib Ullah, Agricultural Inspector, Kargil District, Ladakh

the mountains to the south, cascading majestically midst the native deodars (Himalayan cedars). For the first time there was a real warmth about, though this did not extend too far into the shadows. When I judged that I had walked far enough from settlement to be immodest, I stripped and scrubbed my clothes, hanging them on branches to dry in the windy sunshine. Then I returned to bathe in the cold pool and, emerging, lay down upon a large boulder in the full glare of the sun, and drifted off.

It may appear as idleness.
But as I lie here, forgetful
on sun-baked granite,
The same sun melts the snows on the passes
through the mountains which lie before me.

❋   ❋

5.

UPSTREAM

The morning came when we threw our packs onto the roof and settled into the bus to *Panikhar*, forty-five miles to the south, upstream along the *Suru*. Immediately upon leaving Kargil the landscape reverted to barrenness, sleet greyed the day, and the hours passed as the bus ground and lurched forward through the ruts. Once we came to a particularly boggy stretch and the driver considered abandoning the journey, but after consultation with the passengers decided to have a run at it. Later still, a flat tyre provided a needed rest stop, as riding the bus was a full-time job for everyone aboard. People and baggage were spilled out to enable the bus to be jacked up, and we stretched our limbs or reclined in the only sun to shine. It was evening when we reached our destination.

There, amongst the scattered homesteads of Panikhar village, we sought lodgings before dark would fall. This time it was poor fortune though, as no sooner had we prepared our beds for the night on the dirt floor of our guesthouse room that the atrabilious cook thrust some cold and miserable fare before us – unidentifiable colourless lumps suspended in congealed gum rubber. So after a small bite from our own store we went for a stroll under the first stars.

The good bus had delivered us to a much greater elevation than Kargil, and the surrounding glaciers here sharpened and scented the valley's night air. As we admired the starlit surrounds, we were joined in silhouette by Gulam Rasool, who introduced himself as a local mountaineering guide. Gulam very graciously invited us back to his family's home, where his mother proceeded to send up course after sumptuous course, alternating warm and spicy wholesomeness with palate-clearing and cooling *crudités*. Gulam's friend "Johnny" joined us. From New Delhi, Johnny's task was to oversee licensed climbing expeditions on behalf of the Indian government. We talked into the night about their climbs of Nun and Kun, the twin-peaked massif over the ridge to the east, and of weather and terrain. As Gulam brokered pack animals for these expeditions, we mentioned the matter of a horse, and he said he would put the word out locally. With *adieu* we made our way back through the cold night to our dusty earthen floor.

The main route to Zanskar proceeds beyond Panikhar, following the Suru through a sharp cleft in the wider landscape, in which this significant river nearly doubles back upon itself to the northwest. Gulam had told us of a path up over the sharp ridge which bisected this meander. Though unsuitable for equestrian use, it would offer us a day's walk and enable us to view the landscape ahead. After preparing and consuming lashings of porridge, we set off across the river and some time later we had left the valley floor far behind. Scrambling up a final incline, the abrupt summit revealed foreground eagles soaring upon a thermal against a backdrop of the full majesty of the Nun-Kun massif, her glaciers peaking into the cobalt blue of rarefied air. We could now clearly see that, to reach the Kingdom of Zanskar, we would have to skirt this massif, taking the Suru to its source over several days' walk, and thence over the Pensi-la, at fourteen thousand odd feet the lowest point along the considerable ridge which here presented itself. From the current vantage we viewed these daunting mountains which lay before us with equal parts of awe, trepidation and a strong desire to enter them.

Returning to the valley floor in the afternoon, we found that Gulam had organised a veritable horse fair for our benefit. Over the course of an hour or so, several worthy beasts were paraded by and offered to us – a mare with a gambolling foal, another in young and about to drop, still another showing. We settled

"To reach the Kingdom of Zanskar, we would have to skirt the Nun-Kun massif, taking the Suru to its source..."

on a stallion, though he was nearly withdrawn when Gulam translated a remark from Paddy which suggested that, as the horse was a bit thin, shouldn't the price reflect this and come down a few rupees? In all fairness, there is a paucity of feeding there in the late winter and early spring, with everybody showing a few ribs at this time, and two considerations were beyond question: the legendary stamina of these tough little ponies, and the integrity of the vast majority of these mountain people.

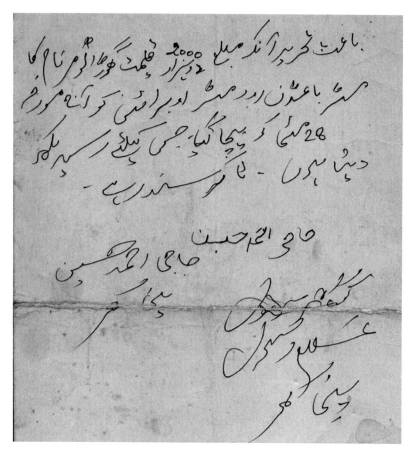

"Deed of Sale for the Horse formerly known as Tomer"
("It is agreed that I am going to sell the horse named Tomer to Mr. Kai and Mr. Li of Ireland which costs Rupees 2000/ with saddle, belt, blanket and bridle. – Haji Hussein of Panikhar")

The deal was made, duly recorded in Urdu and translated into English. We were now the owners of the white stallion known as "Tomer", who we rechristened "Himself".

The following morning saw my prophetically bespoke muslin saddlebags fitted upon Himself and, following an equitable distribution of loads we, now three, turned our gazes further upstream. Cold, lonely days followed. The blizzard would rise, and as visibility came down to a few yards, Paddy and I would exchange wondering glances through frosted beards and iced brows. When we could go no further, the horse would be tethered and blanketed, with hay, which we had carried with us, spread before him. The tent would be pitched, and as the snow rose around it, we would make tea inside on the primus and tell stories as the wind raged. Morning, midday and evening one of us would roll up a dough ball with barley flour and raw cane sugar and feed it to Himself. Then the storm would abate and we would make another few miles.

After four days, the morning came when, opening the tent flap, I was greeted by an abandoned tether. Paddy headed back down, and I up the valley, but when we met at noon neither of us had had any luck. Then something caught Paddy's eye, and he gestured to a tiny white speck high upon the mountainside. Careful study revealed that it was in fact moving about, though by the time we gained his station and convinced Himself to re-join us the day was done, and any progress would have to wait until another day.

Because of the poor status of geographical information about the region at that time, we had only a notion of where we were and how far we must trod to gain a given destination. I'm not saying that we cared much about this state, but when we came across an extremely remote and unexpected settlement the following day, and not knowing the duration of what lay before us, we decided to accept an offer to resupply our provisions. This was in the form of a crude but welcome bag of *tsampa* (roast, ground barley flour), more than a kilo, which our hostess in this nameless place was willing to sell us for a few Indian rupees.

As we were halted, she tilted back her *perak* (the customary Tibetan married woman's hat, brimmed with a long tailing duck-bill laden with all of the precious stones she possesses) and succoured us with tea and a sample of the *tsampa*. We concluded the deal, expressed our appreciation at her graciousness as best as we were able, and pushed on. This was my first encounter with *tsampa*. Perhaps I did not dilute it with sufficient tea, or ate it too fast, but walking on, my gut said "What?!?" and gradually began to seize and I could go no more. All night and through the next day I suffered with a knot of barley flour lodged in my stomach which, after a full day camped with any thought of progress abandoned, finally dissolved (Allah/Buddha/Jehovah be praised), and I became mobile again.

Fresh fodder became scarce as the valley rose and we climbed back into winter, rare patches of green giving way to simple and clean geologic freshness, imposing bare rock faces filling the valleys with alluvial fans of pure scree. For the sake of Himself we would detour miles for a single blade of grass. Perseverance through the wind eventually brought us to the plain of Rungdum. Here, where the Suru accepts a tributary, the valley widened considerably.

In the midst of this expansive floor, founded on a solitary drumlin, sits the *gompa* (Tibetan Buddhist temple and lamasery) of the same name, a diverting medieval mirage after our days of snow and loneliness. Six lamas who had noticed our approach greeted us outside the lamasery gates. Two of them led Himself away for a feed of barley straw, and I was pleased to see him stalled out of the elements. The other lamas insisted that we come for a tour of the *gompa*, so keen both to share it with us and to see their lamasery through our eyes. I hope that we did not disappoint them.

Paddy and I were in awe at the world into which we had just walked, and this was to be the beginning of our realisation of this fact. The lamas' easy gestures, and tones that echoed like ventriloquists off of clay walls which had always been there, were enough to suspend time, and we took to their ancient milieu. We were conducted into a claustrophobic inner temple where the darkness enhanced the pungent musk/ rancid-buttery pall. As the eyes adjusted, dim lines of gold leaf dawned out of a deep recess behind a shrine, revealing the outlines of a large statue of the Enlightened One. Though no monk was chanting, there was yet a sense of ceaseless cymbals, horns and gongs.

Returning into the flat sunlight, they took us around to a roofed balcony. Paddy and I were struggling to comprehend the Tibetan dialect, but it was not difficult to grasp how much they cherished the fresco of Padmasambhava (the venerated Saint who brought Buddhism to Tibet from the sub-continent), which had been lovingly painted there under the colonnade. Though Zanskar proper still lay a few more days' walk over the mountains, Rungdum, as an outpost, shaped our wondrous welcome to the kingdom.

Pensi-La is the lowest saddle in the redoubtable Zanskar Mountains at this point, and offers the only practical portal into the heart of the Kingdom. With a farewell to our hosts in Rungdum *gompa*, our ascent of Pensi-la began on a clear, bright morning, but as we steadily gained in elevation the afternoon greyed, and crystals began to dance and twirl on an indecisive wind. Visibility came down to but a few yards, as the earth became ever harder and more brittle. With no reference points it was like sleepwalking in a cloud. We wondered at our bearings, but persisted as we didn't care to stop – the snap of an arctic breeze forbade any possibility of breaking for tea, demanding only that we continue our exertions merely to sustain sufficient body heat.

Did "hours" pass as an immeasurable ascent was sustained throughout a day which will never come again? Our rhythmical steps through the undifferentiated grey created a hypnotic state that seemingly ruled out the possibility that we may ever achieve some resolution. But finally the climb levelled a bit, and like awakening after years we rose up out of the frozen fog and into searingly brilliant sunlight which uplit the stratospheric blue of a late afternoon, though the billows still obscured the valley out of which we had just so laboriously arisen. We espied a small stone shelter, made our way over to inspect it, and knew what we had to do.

It was half-roofed with massive corbelled flagstones, and had a small adjacent cubicle for animals. Himself was relieved of his pack, and we turned him loose in a lush patch of unexpected (for the summit!) grass in the midst of the snow field. We moved in and set up housekeeping out of the gale. Paddy had a touch of elevation sickness, so I made him get into his sleeping bag and rest, while I made oat and apricot porridge on the primus. This complaint can affect anyone at altitude, and I assumed that we had risen from around eight thousand feet to well over fourteen thousand over the course of our unbroken day-long climb. Where any more than minor symptoms appear, the only treatment is a rapid descent. Naturally enough, we both hoped to avoid this option.

Pensi-la was to be the first, and one of the least, of many ascents which lay in the mountains ahead. Paddy was stable though, and when I saw that he was comfortable as well, I strolled over and sat by a low cairn to pack a celebratory pipe and survey our surrounds. The stones which formed the cairn are carried up here by passing travellers, who commission craftsman-lamas to carve prayers in Tibetan script upon them. When added to the cairn, these prayers and images bless the traveller, his journey and indeed all sentient beings. And for me these ideograms provided an ineffable caption for the absolute wilderness which we had now entered.

"The stones which form the cairn are carried up here by passing travellers, who commission craftsman-lamas to carve prayers in Tibetan script upon them."

The fantastical cloud was being spawned in the unfathomable chasm below and borne aloft by a steady updraught. Beyond our station, however, this condensation could not be sustained and, to gain orientation, I strained against the sun's flare to peer through the waving wisps which forested the cloud top (just below me!). There were hints of distant glaciers, and the sharp black shadows of their peaks advanced through this raging spectral sea.

Suddenly, and incredulously, the wind ceased and, before my eyes, the remaining cloud evaporated in entirety with an audible hiss. I could now look down upon the cavernous reaches of the gorge which we had blindly straddled all day, and, about me, the splendour of an earth full of snowy summits and saddles extending to all points. As the ragged horizon eclipsed the full sun I went and fetched Himself, led him back to a ration of hay, and ensured that he was securely stalled for the night, as we had been warned of the danger of bears killing horses up here. Paddy was tired but felt much better.

Dusk was passing quickly, so I readied my bed. With the wind gone, there was an intense silence, save for the horse's calm ruminations which I could hear through the chinks in the wall which separated us. From our cocoons we could gaze up through the circled silhouette which framed an aperture in the stone roof, and there, Jupiter and Saturn in conjunction leapt out from a backdrop of dense empyrean clusters.

❋　　❋

6.

INTO THE ICE

We slept through the clear, cold night and awoke to the crack of a distant avalanche. As the myriad mountains worked through a palette of dawn blushes we broke camp and headed off into the ice. Along the summit of the Pensi-la, we were on the spine of the Zanskar Range. These mountains are drier and more jagged (ice-chipped rather than water-worn) than the Himalayas, which they parallel in northwest-southeast aspect. This is due to the monsoons and general weather patterns which, arising out of the Indian Ocean, sweep across the subcontinent – rising, cooling, condensing, spawning the rain forests and lushness of the foothills, climbing still higher and depositing heavy snows on the main Himalayas. But this act leaves the clouds spent, with little more than an annual dusting of snow to sustain Zanskar's glaciers, and rendering her abyssal valleys as virtual deserts.

At last we descended out of the whitened earth, past frozen pools which are the source of the Doda River. In the cliffs above caves and the occasional hut were visible, which we later learned were the abodes of meditating lamas. Late morning was warming as we left the stony pass. Himself, with a snort and a whinny, seemed to express pleasure at being on level ground once more. As we progressed, just before us a *tourbil-lion* was spontaneously born out of the windless day, drifted across the valley and was spent as quickly, yet seemed to herald the approach of a lone rider from across the plain ahead. As he came upon us, in a single movement he dismounted, bowed and uttered a guttural welcome. His countenance featured eyes like turquoise which had been set in leather. In a clipped Zanskari dialect he confirmed our bearings, wished us every happiness, remounted and, with an air of urgency, galloped off into the mountains from which we had just emerged.

As ever, grazing dictated our place of rest, so we stopped to cook a meal in a relatively verdant arroyo cut into the valley floor. The etch of the bed suggested that the midsummer sun sends torrents of glacier melt-off through here but now, as winter was only beginning to yield, Himself was set free to munch the low grass. Paddy made *chapattis* while I looked after a rice and onion dish, flavouring it all with a quantity of hot pickle. We reclined on our saddlebags while the little fire for the kettle died away, sipped a contemplative cup of tea on the frozen earth, and scanned the landscape: the withered river bed, the serrated walls of the arroyo, then raising my eyes to the wind-chiselled spires and beyond, the purposeless cirrus. Distilled stillness, yet still a pulse to the silence.

The following day, though we were still high in the Doda Valley, we came across the first Zanskari village, with well-spaced houses amidst the terraced tundra fields. We were greeted by a middle-aged woman in a black corduroy over-garment and worn felt hat and boots who hailed us, "*Cha, cha?*" ("Tea, tea?"). Himself was relieved of his burden, stanchioned with some hay, and we ourselves were led to a small, low-walled area adjacent to the dwelling. In the strained brilliance of the

"We broke camp and headed off into the ice..."

early spring afternoon, it made a pleasant sun trap. One of her husbands joined us (Zanskar is polyandrous – more anon), and cup after cup of buttered and salted tea was poured, then *tsampa* offered around. Again, following their example, we stirred the meal into a half-drunk cup of tea to make a gruel, and scooped it out with twinned fingers to eat it. Another cup of tea was poured, again the *tsampa* mixed with the green twig tea (like Japanese *bancha* tea) for a further round, and this was repeated until satiation.

The strong mutual curiosity found expression in simple discourse, Paddy's and my slim Tibetan precluding any other topics save for universal concerns of weather, the mode and cost of transport, where we are coming from, and where we are going. A boy of about nine emerged from the house and, leaning against the adobe wall, listened to our chat. Listened, but not watched, as his eyes were swollen tight and encrusted with dried mucous. I attempted to learn why he was in such an appalling state, and slowly I pieced together that he had been indoors for the harsh winter and therefore had spent months in the acrid smoke of the dung and twig cooking fires. There was no chimney! Indeed, none of their neighbours had chimneys as they deemed it to be too much of a heat loss. The consequence of being confined inside during the harsh winter was, "Sure, all of the children suffer this condition" by winter's end. I was outraged, though it was not merely my tenuous grasp of the language which made me hold my tongue. For me, it remains a conflict when travelling: to simultaneously be, on the one hand, receptive to and empathetic with one's host, no matter what his culture and station, whilst on the other to condemn ignorance and the roots of suffering wherever and whenever they arise. At least one should dwell in clarity, without idealising or despising those about you. Nevertheless, I was still shaking my head as I led our fed and watered pony from the village.

Between villages we produced another bivouac under the stars, and the following day found us well down the easy ambling descent of the Doda Valley. Villages, and local travellers, became more frequent, and a pleasant easing of the weather was picked up by a theme of cheerful salutations along the way. Our humour sprouted in response, and why wouldn't it? The three of us were fresh, life is long. Though the path was hard we were gay and if we had a destination, it could wait.

Not long after midday we made a stop in the village of Phe, where we were placed on felt mats and succoured by a farmer cum merchant-traveller of that village. His generous kaftan, a locally woven outer woollen garment, redoubled his robustness, and he laughed and farted over our opening remarks, then proceeded to serve us with a wonderful attentiveness and delicacy. *Thugpa* (fresh rolled wheat pasta in a dried mutton-based stock) and *chang* (beer) were placed upon the low Tibetan table before us. Passionate to learn the dialect, the meal was punctuated by one of us gesturing to, or handling something, and asking its name. It was the source of much entertainment, with our host alternately roaring with laughter or nodding thoughtful approval at something deep and profound which we had inadvertently uttered.

A suitable lull in this discourse provided the moment for him to turn to the elaborate and vigorous task of tea-brewing. This extraordinary tea-making ritual is followed by the consumption of copious amounts. Liquid is doubly so the essence of the diet here, as between the zero humidity and the parched wind, dehydration may occur long before thirst, with dire consequences. (Years later I cannot see a reference to this land without feeling the skin tighten across my cheeks in response to the memory of aridity.)

Others have quite correctly described the salted, buttered Tibetan tea as being more like a *bouillon*. The savoury broth is the welcome antidote to the demands of the environment. For the final course our companion drew a cotton bag of *tsampa* from within his capacious garment and, releasing its ties, offered it around. We gratefully mopped up the last of the tea with this gruel. "Grainy" does not half describe the smoky barley/pea flour mix. It is gritty, edible, *palatable* earth, and I can only begin to imagine the strength of stalk which the young shoots around Phe will have when harvest time comes, as it tastes of ancient grain, and I wondered at, but was unable to pursue, its husbandry and basis for selection.

Apart from offering coarse nutrition, Paddy and I both enjoyed the *tsampa* and, in a final attempt at conversation, sought to describe (in faltering demi-Tibetan) the subtler qualities of various blends we had sampled thus far. This exchange once more broke down into tears of mirth, and our host bundled us back out the door and on our way, but not before bidding us a warm goodbye and indicating that the Karsha *gompa* was now within our compass and would surely welcome us.

Below Phe village the valley opened up more, and as we faced downstream to the southeast, we could see that there was a cleft to the north, and the shadows of a deeper valley arcing away to the south. Our map-making efforts suggested that this must be the confluence of the Doda, from the northwest, and the Tsarap, from the southeast, becoming one and turning to the north as the Zanskar River. In the five mile wide plain formed by this junction lay the heart of the Kingdom of Zanskar, with its greatest concentration of population distributed amongst half a dozen villages (together with their lamaseries) within sight of each other scattered across the wide valley floor.

7.

THE KINGDOM

Extending shadows outpaced us on the other side of the valley. Rounding the sweep in the range, we reached the village of Karsha, and there paused to gaze up the cliffs to the Lamasery of the same name before ascending. At the top of the steep switch-backed path we arrived at the gates and were hailed by a fresh-faced monk in his mid-twenties who was on his way down for water. He introduced himself as Lobsang Tchamchoops, and he would be delighted if we shared his apartment with him. He admired our stallion as he led Himself to the stables just inside the gate, and placed some really grand (alfalfa!) hay before him. Then we were shown through the opening courtyard and up, up twisting stone steps, rising past tiers of buildings, which in their cluttered geometry resembled the replicating cells of some weird crystalline growth clinging to the side of the mountain.

Lobsang produced a key of sorts and opened a wooden lock. We stepped through a dark passageway, past his teacher's quarters, then up a stairwell which led out on to a balcony which commanded a view of the central plain and surrounding peaks, so vast and awe-inspiring that it stopped us in our tracks. Lobsang drew near, and perhaps in his familiarity with

*"We reached the village of Karsha, and there paused to gaze
up the cliffs to the Lamasery of the same name ..."*

the environs was curious at our powerful reaction to it. He then
gestured to a small room off to one side where we might stow
our gear and sleep, and then disappeared into a small kitchen
on the other side of the balcony to prepare tea.

Paddy and I returned to the view. From Lobsang's eyrie, we
looked down the cliff face, which was whitened and cubed by
the Lamasery clinging to it. From the base of this, we could
see the houses of the village spaced here and there amidst the
terraced fields, which spread in a fan for at least half a mile,
before lapsing to the unirrigated stone and silvered sienna of
the valley floor. Some miles away one could make out that the
Zanskar River cut a gorge in the middle of this. From the far
side of the valley the mountains rose abruptly until their frozen crowns presided over scattering nimbus. We were fatigued
from our days walking and nights camping. Now we were

roofed and welcomed, and could allow our gazes to wander without purpose.

There followed many pleasant and edifying days in Karsha Lamasery. Lobsang sustained us with his roasted flat wheat breads, *tsampa*s, and extraordinary stewed *thugpa*s, prepared with *kumuk*, which we had seen starting to appear with late spring as a low, earth-hugging and, for here, fairly leafy plant which is used as a fresh or cooked green vegetable (in Ireland it is known as "famine weed"). A portion of every dish prepared was served up into an old hollowed burl of walnut, which he would take down the darkened stairwell to his teacher-Lama who resided in the apartment below. We learned that to become a full Lama, like his revered teacher, one had to matriculate through many varied passages, including demonstrations of spiritual wisdom and solitary meditation for three years, three months and three days, and that this course was not necessarily completed within the span of a single lifetime.

Paddy and I continued to acquire the rudiments of the Zanskari dialect of Tibetan which is spoken here. Wishing to be fluent, we applied ourselves assiduously to its practice by sunlight or butter lamp, and agreed to keep our own, unpressing, conversations to this medium. The denizens of Karsha were engaged: idle Lamas were cornered, and they obliged with light-hearted discussion; dogs were addressed in their native tongue. I filled sheets of rice paper with my note-taking. Vocabulary swelled and understanding dawned!

❋   ❋

A path wended away around the south face of Karsha Lamasery's ridge and dropped into a gorge. There below, aside the stream, I found the most wondrous little machine. A small amount of flow had been diverted and channelled by a hollowed log, which directed this flow upon wooden paddles wedged into a timber axle. This powered a crankshaft which was frantically driving a block of wood over a coarse surface of flat granite, gradually rendering the small log into sawdust. A measured amount of water constantly rinsed the granite, and gathered the red to purple dust into a muslin trap. The device's felt-aproned operator was perched above his charge on a rock in the late morning sun, and from time to time leapt down to stop it and replace some piece which had fallen off. With his intense preoccupation I had gone unnoticed. I was slow to approach him for fear of distracting him, but eventually I weakened and hailed him above the stream's rush to inquire of his task. His reply was a courteous but necessarily brief shout that the aromatic dust contributed a factor to incense making, and that, to learn more, I should speak with Lama Rabtan, who is the Chief Incense Maker of the Lamasery.

In the afternoon I found Lama Rabtan holding court (could one say a gaggle of lamas?) within a colonnade in front of his own apartment. With my arrival, they one by one all passed some jest at my expense, though now I was becoming just fluent enough to enable me to good-naturedly point out a few of their own deficiencies by way of stuttered reply. These exchanges bonded us to the extent that I was thrown down upon a mortar bench and invited to speak my mind. When I revealed that my interest was the Lama's incense-making there followed a very enthusiastic lecture upon the subject. Producing a roll of his own making, he picked it apart with a substantial thumbnail and identified the various constituent flecks as *fuekar* (charcoal), *larsee* (musk), *akir* (juniper) – I'm afraid the rest of it escaped me, but if incense is meant to assist the transcendental, this seemed to be the recipe. He thrust it into some embers glowing in a brazier and waved it under my nose. With my eyes closed it was exotic, yet familiar. There was then, however, a curious interjection. A dark Lama, who had before said nothing amidst all of the exchanges, suddenly sprang to approach me from his perch in the shadowed colonnade and, as savant and seer, proclaimed that I had lived here before, in a past life. A mole on the side of my torso, which he could not have known about, would prove this, as I had been a low-ranking deity with six arms previous to that! The group fell into a hush, glanced at each other, conducted a clipped guttural conference, and then commenced to tease me with a new vigour, maintaining, in hysterics, that I had been going downhill for quite a long time. Feebly, I could muster no defence.

I was reclining on a thick felted bunk in our little doorless room, daubing some watercolour into my latest map, when Lobsang's Lama appeared on the balcony with a stone, hammer and chisel, a bowl of water, and some vermilion dust. With a brief and mumbled greeting he ignored me and, settling himself upon a mat, gave the stone a wash with the dissolved vermilion, and proceeded to chink away at it. I returned to my map-making and, after two hours, as I blew upon the map to dry my daubed tawny elevations, he had the sacred characters (*om mani padme hum*) carved in the stone. My map would not assist me – through serendipity I had found my Way (God bless all who may follow). But his finished stone would be carried aloft by a devotee to join one of the long *mani* walls, or the *chortens* (cairns) which mark the summits of passes, and thereby guide and sanctify the route of believers and dissenters equally.

Paddy and I had a chance meeting with the Abbot of Karsha, a brother of the Dalai Lama, in one of the near vertical "streets" of the Lamasery. Lacking a scarf or some such token for the traditional presentation upon meeting one of high rank, the quick thinking Paddy dove into his coat pocket and, with all pomp and a courteous bow, handed him a paper bag of cinnamon rock sweets (borne all the way from Cork City!) which the Abbot graciously received in an alcove into which we had stepped.

One evening we were sitting on the balcony with Lobsang having a calm post-prandial chat when I asked him about his watch, the hands of which had not appeared to progress in all of the sublime days we had passed in his company. An explanation was given: ever since photographs had appeared of the Dalai Lama wearing glasses and a watch, there had apparently been a wave of interest in acquiring these effects (lens prescriptions or time of day notwithstanding). Would Lobsang care for me to take his watch with me on my wanderings, which should probably lead me to Leh (capital of Ladakh to the north, where there is surely a watchmaker?), and return it mended when I hoped to pass through Zanskar again in a month or two? Lobsang's eyes drifted across the landscape as he contemplated the likelihood of this scenario, then they returned to his watch. He undid the strap and handed it to me. I carefully wrapped it and put it in my pack.

❋　　❋

We decided to walk to Padum, effectively the capital of Zanskar, and stay a night. It lies within our view from here, five miles across the plain, just where the River Tsarap emerges from its shadowy blue-black canyon. We had planned on visiting Padum on our way south in several weeks' time. Thinking, however, that our rice and various other stocks may not last the trek north to the Indus (through quite desolate regions), this was a good opportunity to resupply as well as have one look at the civic centre of Zanskar.

With Himself in Lobsang's care, we left the Lamasery at noon one day, and went down through the village and along the sluice-bordered fields just sprouting their wheat and barley. Leaving the fields behind, we walked the hard earth until we reached the main river, then turned upstream beyond the meeting of the rivers so that we might only ford what the Doda contributed. At least it was still fordable, forsaking only our trousers to nimbly wade through the freezing dark water. Drying off and on our way, we moved through Pipiting village, with its wonderful *chorten* perched upon a high granite outcrop which had resisted the meanders of the aeons and seemed to be in so many ways the centre of the valley. It was evening when we arrived in Padum, and we sought accommodation for the night.

We were taken in by a family and given their newly built extension as our quarters. We were stowing our gear when a young lad arrived with an invitation to join the three resident Kashmiri civil servants for dinner. This proved to be a treat. They had trained the lad to prepare their *garam masalas*, and these he served with more rice than I had ever seen, *dal* (spiced lentils), and some tinned *subje* (vegetables), followed by a fingerbowl, and we delighted in speaking English with our loquacious hosts. Though learned and capable of real largess, they were generally miserable, cut off from their young wives and having to spend one to three years of their fledgling careers being India's bureaucratic vanguard in these mountains, with only their curries to look forward to. One had a beautiful voice, and he sang freely for us.

When decorum suggested we make away, we arose, stretched and, thanking them, walked homewards through the starlit streets. But I got an urge to explore, so I told Paddy that I would meet him back at our digs. Parting, I rounded a corner, keeping a hand on the walls to stay myself on the dark uneven ground, and discovered that I was in a small plaza, in the centre of which was a *chorten* (sacred geometric statuary representing the five constituent elements of earth, water, fire, air and aether). I was admiring its silhouette against the firmament, and gazed up at Jupiter and Saturn, in conjunction, just south of directly overhead. I heard a rustle and the sound of felted footsteps approaching, and was addressed by an elderly Tibetan voice: "What are you looking at?"

"*Spinba* and *Purbu*," I replied, indicating the two planets with my chin. He joined me in the view and, after awhile, remarked more or less that they were exceedingly beautiful to behold. He seemed delighted with my knowledge of the planet's (Tibetan) names, and asked me to enumerate the remaining (visible) planets. When I had effectively recited the days of the week, and we had dispensed with the inevitable "where are you coming from, where are you going?", he said that he was at my service and that he would assist me in any way he could.

I mentioned that I understood that Padum was the seat of the *Gyalpo* (King) of Zanskar, and perhaps he would point out the King's house as I had hoped to call on him at some opportunity. He replied that that was the smallest thing that I could ask of him and bade me to follow. Follow I did, but barely, for despite his apparent age he ducked under arches, squeezed down alleys, dove through apertures, and generally threaded his way through this starlit labyrinth so quickly that I could hardly stay with him. Finally, he disappeared through a low door. In the darkness a donkey sneezed. I followed the sound of his footfalls up uneven stone steps, out again under the stars on to a roof top patio, across to a single room built onto the roof's corner. Inside, my guide struck a light to a butter-lamp and, as it lit up his wonderfully wizened Mongol face, he leaned across and said simply, "I am the King". My grasp of the dialect was now sufficient for me to be speechless in two languages.

❋   ❋

With morning I had a glimpse upstream along the River Tsarap, the route which, in another season, might bring us over the main Himalayas through Shingo-la and into the northern Indian state of Himachal Pradesh. The aspect of the canyon cradled the rising sun, and though I knew it led to glaciated fastness, it seemed inviting. I returned to explore Padum by day, and then we had to attend the granary where, as travellers to the north, we were allowed a good ration.

Back through the village again I met Katcho Isfandyar Khan, the enlightened face of the Jammu and Kashmir agricultural advisory presence. An invitation followed to take tea in his dak bungalow-style quarters, which are set apart from, and conspicuous in contrast to, the organic clay evolution of Padum's architecture. Katcho told of the success of the new willow and poplar plantations, and the contribution this timber crop was making to life in this branchless desert. He was full of energy and good will with regards his duties there. The Kingdom proper dissolved with India's independence, and it is from this building that India administers Zanskar. One could shudder at the imposition of new techniques and values upon a society which had survived along proven lines for so long. However, if India's intentions remain as benevolent as the agricultural advisor's, and Zanskar's well-being the cornerstone of the mission, then the contact may be mutually beneficial. Only time will tell.

In the afternoon, laden with our fresh *tsampa* flour, we headed back across the expansive plain. The Karsha *gompa* loomed in the distance, perched upon its crag. There was a good chance Lobsang would have the kettle on. Li Tai Po (Paddy), for his part, had dismissed my account of the meeting with the King, and admonished me for my nocturnal wanderings. The invitation to be the King's guests on our return journey stood, however, and I was sure that we would avail of it on our way south, in another season.

8.

CURIOSITY CALLED US ALONG

Daybreak saw the knot cinched on the pony's load. Lobsang Tchamchoops bade us (and his watch) farewell from the main gates of Karsha *gompa*. We turned north along the Zanskar River, and in the gently rising valley floor we had sufficient breath to discourse. "Shorten the road!" Paddy encouraged, and imaginary tales were bartered. Our hopes for this first day back on the road extended only as far as Pishu.

Entering that hamlet after noon we were greeted by a man sitting at an outdoor loom, hands and feet occupied in warp and weft. He looked up with the unvarying greeting: "Where are you coming from, where are you going, and what did you pay for your horse?" Having answered these queries as accurately as possible, we then examined his clever loom, before wishing him the very best and taking our leave. Further along we met another villager who told us that we must go admire the extraordinary bridge (*zamba*) which spanned the main Zanskar gorge. We decided that we couldn't miss this, so beyond the village we pitched our tent and tethered Himself with access to some fodder. We then headed back towards the main gorge to find the bridge.

Coming upon it, we were agog at this engineering feat. It is an eighty yard span, consisting of willow twigs bound together in three *sugan* cords, one to step upon, the other two at chest height to hold on to, slung between massive stone anchorages on either bank. The three parallel salix cables are lashed together with more willow diagonals, and, swaying and sagging, the bold structure dips within four or five feet of the mid-river's current. We crossed one at a time, not wishing our combined weight to overstretch the twigs. As guinea pig-in-chief I picked my way across it, Paddy content to hang behind with the camera trained on my progress, before he too gamely crossed.

Zangla village, as we had been told, the seat of a former Zanskar king, was a small stretch further along, so curiosity called us along to view it. A village in Zanskar is not peopled in the manner that one may find in other lands – it is a severely restricted population, and necessarily so, but entering within its adobe-like structures there was no one to be seen. A short reconnoitre revealed a collection of proud and pleasing homes, the flat roofs capped with hoards of hard-won bundles of twig firewood.

We turned to leave, but only in departing were we finally hailed from a doorway by an attractive woman in *perak* and a heavily-woven black wool dress, who gestured for us to enter. We were conducted up the stairs into the main room of the house, where her husband, with a lovely baby girl nestled in one arm, was seated upon the earthen floor, stirring barley-corns which he was roasting in a shallow copper pan over a dung and twig fire. There is no glass in Zanskar. A window-like aperture had been cleared of the clay bricks which had closed it for the winter, and now the afternoon sun's rays cut through the peat-like smoke which filled the room.

The man smiled up at us as we entered and, as the barley was done to a turn, he set the swaddled child upon the earthen floor, removed the pan from the fire, raked the embers together, and began the tea-making sequence. The bustle woke the child, but she just stared serenely at us from within her swathe. Li Tai Po and Kai Lung were invited to recline, and conversation began to unfold.

We were curious about the bridge, and our host informed us that its maintenance is carried out in winter, when scaffolding may be erected on the frozen river. And, of course, that there is no need for the bridge in winter, as trails and bridges alike are abandoned for the far more level paths over the frozen watercourses. He was obsessed with the river, and told us with some feeling of the efforts of the Lamas in rescuing trout which would be stranded in small pools, forgotten by the shrinking torrent when autumn came.

The boiled kettle was emptied over tea leaves to steep. Our hostess disappeared for a moment and returned from a neighbouring house with her sister in tow. After an introduction, she reheated the tea over the embers, and then poured it into a churn before adding a measure of yak butter and salt. She then proceeded to vigorously plunge the churn until she was happy, and then returned the brew to the kettle for a final reheating.

On a sign from her eyes we produced our cups to be filled. Oh this was delightful tea. We had tasted enough now to compare and contrast the subtleties. The liquor was well-judged, the salt rightly stated and the butter was fresh, with a long finish that wrapped the pallet in luxuriousness without being too cloying! This assessment, of course, was all an aside between

Paddy and myself; our message to our hosts was that the tea was without equal. And, as *tsampa* was combined with subsequent cups and the child was fed some fingered gruel, the conversation was refuelled.

I had noted that the sister had a slight limp as she entered, and this turned out to be the reason she had been produced. Did we have any advice or, better yet, a cure, for her game leg? Paddy, in response, was only too happy to roll up his trouser leg to display the elastic employed to support his own dodgy knee. A startled gasp arose from our friends – even the child sat up – as there is no living skin quite so pale as the Celtic skin. They had only encountered this whiteness of flesh with their own dead, and were completely taken aback by the sight of Paddy's ivory patina. But they had calmed down by the time he had undone the bandage and offered it to the sister, which she accepted.

Under Paddy's direction, she gathered her dress and commenced to bind the bandage around her own weak knee. An ensuing round of nervous laughter set the cure in motion as we emptied our cups. The sun was nearing the horizon of the south westerly mountains and, as we hadn't checked Himself in some hours, and that a fair scramble back up to Pishu awaited us once more across the river, we thanked our hosts for their kindness, and headed back down to recross the extraordinary Zangla zamba.

Our horse, of course, was just fine, and as we ourselves were sated by the recent repast, I headed back into Pishu village for another look at the hamlet's attractively diminutive *gompa*. There I met the weaver who, having abandoned his task, was leaning against a wall in the lingering dusk, talking with another man. When he saw me he hailed, "Where is your horse?"

For a laugh I took some loose barleycorns from one pocket, poured them into the other, feigned a whinny from within and, patting the pocket, said in Tibetan, "good horse".

I had become aware of the locals' appreciation of the comic, but this man doubled up and struggled as the guffaws welled up. His face was changing colours like an amorous cock turkey. After a few minutes of this he collapsed on the ground, clutching his sides and gasping for air. I expressed concern, but his companion, who had found my charade reasonably humorous but whose response had run a more measured course, waved me away. After a few more minutes he began to calm a bit, but whenever he glanced up at me, this set him upon further paroxysms. Judging that my presence was inhibiting his recovery, I wished his friend well and retreated from the scene.

❋　　❋

Beyond Pishu, in the late morning, we located a good well at the base of a cliff, just back from the river. Connoisseurs of water that we are, this was reason enough to break for the day and set fresh bivouac. Normally we must gather surface water from the streams, as it was generally clouded with the suspended debris of the fiercely erosive forces of glacier, water and wind above, and must be allowed to stand for a few hours before consumption to enable the shiny bits of feldspar, mica and schist to settle. Otherwise, they can lodge in the gut and cause trouble. Here, however, we could drink freely from this artesian goodness and, in the absence of strict itinerary, had found in its presence sufficient reason to halt.

During the night, there was a thunderstorm up on the ridge. I came out of the tent to see lightning illuminating the snowy peaks rising up behind Zangla village across the river, hanging there like some fantastic *corpo santo*, the thunder taking forever to exhaust its echoes off every face of rock in the valley. A light drizzle on the wind was the first rain we had had in Zanskar.

A bright sunny morning followed, though wisps of cloud veiled the heights. Before departing our wondrous well, we filled every container with its luminescent waters to quench us for a few days. Then we journeyed on through the hamlets of Pidmu and Hanumil, without a soul in sight. From there, the path left the valley floor and began rising through stony passages to the pass at Parfi-la. With travellers scarce, we were pleased to meet a Lama and a young boy making their way down towards us. We exchanged, *"Nima gyalyung tokpo chunmo duk"* ("when the sun shines, the streams come flowing"), and the Lama related how this nine-year-old with the remarkable gaze was a reincarnated Lama, and that he was now fit to return to the Lamasery, towards which they were now bound.

As we continued higher the Zanskar River fell away far below us, winding around the cliffs which forced the trail to rise to this height. I led Himself, coaxing him on. Finally, in an avalanche-strewn incline, we were forced to jump from boulder to boulder, straddling a precipice paralleling the river when, in the midst of a leap, the breech rope on Himself snapped and, with the load slipping back around his hind legs, he freaked and reared. I saw it coming but only just, and my blind hand somehow managed to grasp a ledge of granite bedrock. The horse's lead and my full span were violently jerked taut. This checked Himself rearing backwards over the cliff, but turned it into a frenzied hind-legged pirouette which ended in the

"...the Lama related how this nine year old with the remarkable gaze was a reincarnated Lama..."

poor horse collapsing in a panic upon his side. I felt my grip weakening as Paddy produced his knife and bravely dove in amidst flailing hooves to sever the remaining rope and release the saddlebags. Thus unbound, Himself calmly rose and stood

"Trouble on Parfi-la"

there as if nothing had happened. Paddy and I looked down and saw where all of us could have ended.

Somewhat rattled, we gained the pass as evening rose. With a new moon, and a dark night approaching, we forsook enjoying the view in favour of descending quickly to find some level shelter for our camp. We assessed what had gone wrong and saw how we might avoid repetition of such danger. Later, by candlelight in the tent, I kneaded a special mix of barley-meal and raw cane, and took it out to Himself. At such altitude, the firmament is so much more clearly three-dimensional. Jupiter and Saturn remained travelling together against their starscape brocade. Himself finished off his barley ball with careful nibbles as he got near my hand. From below, the shifting light breeze carried the incessant, almost soughing, murmur of invisible rivers, now sounding near, now sounding far, far away.

❉   ❉

9.

TRAVAILS TO THE NORTH

As we peed in the breaking light we were thrilled to see ibex nodding and sniffing above us back on Parfi-La. The overnight breeze, having switched to the south and placing us to their downwind, was the only reason that they had approached so close, as they are the wariest of creatures. Here on this slope balm grew, and a kind of chaparral on which they were obviously hoping to graze. Feeling bad that our presence prevented this, we hastily assembled our kit and dropped down to the Omachu River, just upstream of where it joins the Zanskar.

Here we crossed the stone and cypress-beam bridge which spanned a narrows at the place the denizens call Kutykit (within a wider area known as Snertse), and on to the other side where there was an inviting coppice on a sun-drenched sandy shore. We had not previously come across a garden of this comeliness. Forty dwarf willows had rooted and, with the season, had laid a lush carpet of down. The summer wind had strewn petals of rare briar about the down. The whole scene was absolutely arresting, and we wordlessly broke. Himself was stripped of his burden, and all of our hasty packing was discarded for later inventory. This was not a place to be passed and yet, had we not come upon it, we could never have acknowledged that this is what we sought at that moment. Here we were offered the Earth's hospitality – shelter, beauty, serenity, a neutral place, without social obligation, to calmly be, to lick our wounds, to take stock and to prepare for the more serious passes awaiting us to the north.

Paddy prepared a late breakfast. I led Himself over near to the stoutest tree for support as I got him to give up each hoof for inspection. One shoe had to be removed and refitted. Re-shod, he was patient while I lifted his tail and, finding a leech, fished it out of his arse. After savoury porridge and chapattis, we washed our clothing and, hung over the limbs, it dried in no time in the windy sunshine. Paddy, fastening himself by rope to a bankside willow, lowered himself into the freezing torrent to bathe. Chores done, I had to get the fright of the day before out of me so I got my watercolours out and tried to capture that moment of mayhem on some rice paper.

In the afternoon, our reverie was punctured, not disagree-ably, by the sound of approaching laughter riding over the river's tumbling wash. Three adolescent lads appeared from the northern trail, so taken with their own humour that, com-ing upon us, they howled afresh as if we were the punch line. A greeting of sorts followed, though this was a new dialect (apart from the laughter). Their intentions here were clear, however. Discarding their loads, they dropped to their knees and began collecting rose petals, licking and pasting them to each other's cheeks and brows. After admiring each other, they reshouldered their packs and, laughing, crossed the bridge and climbed away up the south bank.

The remainder of the day passed effortlessly. With time on our hands, and no shortage of fuel here, we cooked a drawn-out evening meal, sautéing onions, garlic, and walnuts in aromatic yak butter, and stirring it all into a big pot of fresh pasta, followed by chapattis served with honeycomb and washed down with black Indian tea. With calm conditions we forsook the tent and spread out our duffle bags upon the broadcast pussy willow, choosing an early night to prepare us for the exertions ahead.

It was not easy to leave the ambience of our willow coppice. From where the Omachu conjoined with the Zanskar River just below our camp, the latter continues northeast to link with the Indus after an eighty-mile plunge through a cliff-bound canyon. This inaccessibility consigns the trail to high ground, with one having to cross five considerable, and a few lesser, mountain passes to gain the Indus at Lamayuru, with this route furthermore linking the northern Zanskari villages.

We had been told that the path, and the immediate pass before us over Hanuma-La to the village of Linshet, was long and arduous. With the weather unpredictable at altitude, and our need to find grazing for Himself, it was important to gain the summit and still have sufficient daylight to allow descent to more temperate habitat. Hence a predawn start to our trek was considered prudent.

We set our faces to the slope, switch-backing a while, finding our breath in the morning frost. With a final glance back down upon Kutykit, we turned and entered a narrow canyon and uncompromisingly kept our pace for several hours. Anyone who has climbed (and most particularly if bearing a load!) knows how difficult it is to surrender the precious rhythm struck up between breath and step. The unknown extent of our travails to the north lent further impetus to hold the pace. Here, some of the more southerly exposed ravine held some shrub, but where the wind lay there was only some hardy and isolated low balm, and finally we climbed beyond vegetation. Clouds didn't gather as such, but a featureless overcast developed as the earth became rock. The temperature plummeted suddenly as we came upon the lower reach of a glacier. Within its icy entrails we could see the boulders being digested into gravel.

We set a course across the frozen meander, and proceeded up for some ways until the horse's hooves began to sound hollow upon the rapidly thinning serac, and at the same moment I spotted an ominous hole in the ice several paces in front of me. Stopping, I knew that we were in a critical situation and, without wanting to alarm Himself, I told Paddy to delicately clear off. To avoid concentrating our combined weight, I played out the full lead and stepped slowly in a wide circle around the horse. Himself complied with a gentle volte-face. Without breathing we retraced our steps until we got over up against the canyon wall where the ice was well founded.

We had mindlessly broken a cardinal rule of transiting unknown icepack: avoid the centre, where the thaw run erodes the structure from underneath! As we reclimbed in safety along the wall, we could then look back inside a spacious ice blue cavern, and be thankful that we hadn't plummeted into it.

Eventually we emerged from the shadowed aspect which conserved this glacier. Here another ravine joined from the north and, as no recognisable path survives the ravages of wind and ice up there (and no hard and fast map existed), we weighed up the likely destination of each. There was no room for error. "The road not taken" is not taken for very good reason. Thankfully, once more we acted with unfailing instinct and chose to fork off into the northern ravine, though the correctness of this course was not to be confirmed for some time yet, until dusk found our hearts bursting as we reached the summit of Hanuma-La. Darkness was not far away, but as it was calm and clear we wished to survey from this vantage. A waxing crescent moon hung away behind us to the southwest. We could make out what must be the village and monastery of Linshet to the north over another minor ridge and into another watershed. Falling sharply away below us was a spread of deep scree. In the bottom of this valley, despite the failing light, we could make out some vegetation. Knowing that this must be our next destination, we set off down the fine gravel, giddy with altitude, the three of us running back and forth across the face of it, our ears popping with the rapid descent. In practised darkness the tent was raised and staked, Himself set free to wander the night by the verdurous brook, and Paddy and I, far too fatigued to prepare food, drifted off into a very deep sleep.

Rising mid-morning, we knew we were in need of some care. Himself whinnied a greeting from down the way, the sway in his gut revealing the extent of his repletion. For us, plenty of buttered porridge from the primus was followed by cups of Indian tea, and this comfort rekindled our morale. I found a frigid pool in which to bathe, then towelled off quickly as the day was harsh and once again overcast.

I took a brisk walk to generate some heat, and then retired to the tent to read and write. We had seen from the top that Linshet lay but a moderate walk away, so it was early afternoon before we set out. Climbing the low pass afforded a view of civilisation in the middle distance, which rose organically up out of a deep chasm through a sylvan plateau and on, becoming a network of terraced fields. Above the fields arose the detached dwellings of the village, and the village in turn was crowned by a whitewashed cellular Lamasery, all set against a draped curtain of soaring granite. Our steps quickened, as we could see we still had a few hours' walk to circuit along a ridge around the western side of the chasm.

An hour later, and about half way around this ridge, we dropped down into an outlying habitation. Spotting us, two husbands and a wife beckoned us to enter their yard, and as we drew up there were offers of *pawa* (bread) and *cha* (tea). Paddy and I glanced at each other, accepted, and Himself was unburdened as water was put to boil. Here however we became uncomfortable. The conversation was strained. They seemed irritable towards each other. The repast was served without sincerity or grace, and we were stunned into silence as we realised what we had walked into. Everywhere we had been welcomed warmly. Everywhere we had made it our business to know what recompense could be fairly offered for hospitality extended, except where payment had been flatly refused. Now these three began to demand roughly eight times more than we had ever been assessed before.

Paddy and I went in to conference. I was incensed but favoured paying them and writing it off. Paddy was livid, and insisted that he would not pay more than three times the going rate of what we had lived with so far. "And," he correctly pointed out, "we stopped only at their persistent entreaty." Counting out so many Indian rupees (which Zanskaris would accept), Paddy handed them to the older husband, who discarded them contemptuously upon the ground. The younger husband began to aggressively root through our bags to discover a more ample bounty, so I moved over and claimed them. It was getting tense. Paddy saddled Himself and started leading him away as I struggled to remonstrate with the three of them, who were turning ugly and threatening. A sudden gust scattered our notes and the elder now dove to claim them. The younger picked up a rock and feigned throwing it at me as I retreated.

With receding qualms we walked our antagonism off, and were nearly gay again by the time we drew level with the Lamasery. From the village a Lama came out to greet us. "Kai Lung? Li Tai Po?" he inquired, as we came within earshot. Word had somehow spread northwards before us as we had travelled from central Zanskar. For his part he related pleasing accounts which had reached him concerning the tales attending these two foreign devils travelling with the white stallion. Himself would spend a few nights indoors with good hay, and we were led to apartments for our use. Our faith in human (and Zanskari) nature was restored by the evening visits of several curious Lamas and villagers. And, we were to have no needs – a wonderful meal of mutton broth, fresh *thugpa*, spring greens and plenty of *tsampa* and tea appeared from the *gompa's* kitchen.

❈   ❈

In Linshet there was opportunity to unpack my swelling notes and, at leisure, to readdress my language studies. It was particularly apropos, as here we found new vocabulary and pronunciation, differing quite noticeably from that in the principle valley to the south. My difficulty demonstrated the role which mountain ranges may play in the restriction of inter-course, leading to the evolution of a distinct dialect. Language, it seems, achieves its own inertial development in valleys, that agreement-of-terms and way-of-putting-things which colours local cultural identity. Language and dialect cross-fertilise by means of the seasonal sprinkling of utterances by such as those attending yak caravans passing through the valley, and of course what they glean and take away with them. What struck me was the enormous contribution which must be made to the creation of dialect by dyslexic travellers.

Tung is one word which remains unchanged throughout this region. It is simple, everyday, and yet exemplifies the in-herent poetic potential. It could mean "partake", or "join to-gether with". Most often it refers to "drink", as in "*cha tung?*" – "will you drink tea?", the *tung*, like nectar, succouring the perpetually dry palate in this desert. And then *tung* might sig-nify "convey", "produce", "emit" or even "anoint". It is at home in many contexts: the term for "music" is *dhamal-soonan tung*, roundly, "drum-flute libation".

Speaking of *tung*, my new acquaintance was asking me about the barley back home. He was curious about what we drink, and full of wonderment at my account of *chang nak-ka*, "black beer", though I avoided revealing the acreage which was used in the production of Irish stout. Two other men stood before us, listening to our chat. They were both con-stantly twirling their small wool spinners. Feeding, weight-ing, gathering, feeding, transforming the *geert-pee* (wool) into *yok-sheen* (finished respun). The talk became sporadic, and toned down with darkness, yet still the two silhouettes blindly spun away.

Dwarf broom had emerged between the sluice borders of the terraced grain crop below Linshet *gompa*. With the higher elevation, the barley grew later here, but established. Three women in *de rigueur* heavy black woollen dresses slowly combed through the crop on their haunches, weeding and loudly chattering away, like benevolent crows tending a crop rather than pilfering it. The late morning sun picked out the gems in their *peraks*, the "dowry" hats with long, trailing, studded brims. One possessed an enormous (and novel) lump of amber set in the field of turquoise and silver ornament.

10.

A Surfeit of Wind

Before us lay another long stretch of country to the north without much habitation. As the glaciers turned magenta, we saddled up and climbed some switch-backs in the steep face which rose straight up behind the Lamasery and, half way up the slope, we met the morning rays coming down. Himself had been gaining weight with the season and some good care. He knew now that he was our horse, and no longer strayed. Paddy and I carried full packs on inclines to ease his burden, and on this morning it became a steep one. By the time we gained Netuksi-La we were just hitting our stride. We were fit and in the prime of life, and we sensed it would be an epic day. Down then, from the first pass into the mountain hamlet of Chumpado-Gongma and it was suddenly summery. Rosemary, daisies wafted on a thermal.

A man was treading his clothes clean in a shallow timber vessel and, as a kettle was just on the boil, he broke for tea with us. And then on we went, up over the further pass of Kuba-la with the sun just past zenith, plunging again, now into a mid-day warmed lower valley of isolated, tiny alpine strawberries, scattered balm, and miniature edelweiss amidst the strewn rock. Here we kindled a quick fire and, just as our tea was brewed, two travellers descended into our camp who we were able to serve. They produced bowls out of their inner sleeves and supped with us, all in agreement about the qualities of the day. I passed about some dried apricots we had carried from Ladakh, lustrous like soft amber. Bowls replaced, they headed off a fork of the trail which led to Yulchung away to the southeast.

Our route, through the pass of Singi-la, rose away to the north. I don't actually recall discussing whether or not to attempt a third considerable climb in the one day. But one moment, we had finished our tea, reclined against our packs, and rested our eyes, and the next, we had wordlessly shouldered our burdens and were again placing one foot before the other. Clearing the rim of this horizonless canyon, our attentions were drawn away up the endless glazed slopes of a nameless pyramid, whose northeast shoulder offered the pass we were seeking. Uniformly rising ground made for an evenly measured, deliberate ascent.

Without further respite we continued for much of the afternoon, until at length we spied the prayer flag-draped cairn, an island in the summit snow pack. With a few hours of daylight still remaining, we felt at some ease to savour the rarefied panorama. Here one could sense the subcontinent colliding with Asia and wrinkling up these peaks. Here one was fraternal with the inaccessible and austere. So Paddy broke out the remains of a Mars bar, which he had been rationing to us for weeks, and carefully pared off another couple of celebratory slices.

"We'll call it Lonely Mountain," proclaimed Paddy, as we regarded the knife-edged white tower looming above us. In rising we had left summer below, and now a frigid downdraft

*"We had risen up out of summer, and now a frigid down-
draft cracked the tattered prayer flags."*

cracked the tattered prayer flags. Below us stretched an un-
populated lunar valley which resolved in an abyssal plunge to
the northeast.

With one eye on the landscape, Himself was reharnessed,
but as we took the first steps in descent through the snow pack
something caught my attention amongst the easy undulations
ranged along the west side of the valley. I drew up and saw that
those distant black specks were a herd of yaks grazing. Being
chief cook, I felt that I could point out to Paddy that we had
now run out of yak butter, and reminded him of the culinary
possibilities which its presence in our larder afforded.

Agreeing coordinates for a likely rendezvous in the lower valley, Paddy took the halter rope and led Himself down, and I set off across the snow field. An hour later I spotted the yaks again at several hillocks distance. Traversing these minor gorges perpendicularly, by the time I rose again they had disappeared. Finally, with dusk closing in on an otherwise endless day, there they were below me.

Seven men were busy tying the yaks' nose-rings to large stones to anchor them for the night. An evening breeze had arisen, so the greeting now was "*Lungs-po mon-po*" ("There is a surfeit of wind"), and a hospitable invitation to tea. I was conducted into their stone summer quarters, so low-ceilinged that the tea churn was operated at an angle. Nightfall was at hand, but one mustn't rush into business, so we exhausted a few subjects before I could even consider mentioning butter (though curiously my sudden appearance in the middle of nowhere was unremarkable). But then two more men appeared at the entrance and, seeing me, could not take their startled gazes off me. It was revealed that these two had not seen a Caucasian before and so now silently crouched near me, weighing my countenance and my tones.

At last we had circled the quarry sufficiently for me to broach the subject. In response, the spokesman reached behind him and produced a stitched yak bladder stuffed with butter. A butter lamp was placed before us on the earthen floor which uplit the huddled conference. Into the wheeling and dealing, an exorbitant amount was put to me, and I replied with a correspondingly undervalued bid. We both warmed to this, and I realised that, given the time it was going to take to bridge this gulf and secure a deal, I might have to pass the night here and look for Paddy in the morning. But he yielded a bit, willingness gradually increased from both sides, back and forth until only a few rupees separated us. Then, however, I determined to take a stand. I thanked them for the refreshing tea and, expressing regret at not striking a deal, crawled outside, bowed and affected an exit. Paddy would be delighted! Alone, and without visible supports, I was going to walk away rather than pay a few extra rupees for the best butter on the planet.

The entire band chuckled at this display of resolve. A mere step later, however, my jovial antagonist called out a final counter. Rounding, I agreed that such an amount would be available if it included a small vessel of curd as well as the butter. Now he clapped his hands with joy, and implored me to come back in and be as one with them. After further rounds of tea to conclude the transaction, I thought that maybe I would try to find Paddy in the starlight. As long as I did not stray too far from the mouth of the ravine, I could always return here to shelter if I failed to find his camp.

So my new-found friends and I parted affectionately and, to my surprise, I found Paddy's bivouac less than a mile away. By the scattered firelight I could see that he was once more rolling out dough and cooking his nourishing flatbreads on the hotplate. Further along, the flickers of flame cast a long dancing shadow of Himself over grass. He looked up, chewing the while. Low gurgles suggested a nearby spring, confirming a sumptuous location. Paddy made room on the fire, and for *hor d'oeuvres* I proceeded to sauté some apricot kernels and carrigeen moss – in yak butter.

Twenty splendid horses, laden with bright multi-coloured woven saddlebags, arrived late the next morning trailed by their three drivers. They halted for grazing and watering, and

I spoke with one of the men. His father was from Tibet and his mother from the northern Indian State of Himachal Pradesh, and he related how he travelled through these mountains in the summer months bearing trade north and south, a mercurial messenger linking his parents' homelands. A likeable shrewdness was written all over his face, and he took a merchant's curiosity in our kit's contents as we packed. Then they took off to the south as we turned north, both parties restored by the grace of one more verdant oasis in the rockscape.

❋ ❋

We knew that only Boumitse-La above lay between us and the village proper. The drover had indicated that Photaksar was not a long walk, so our pace was more leisurely. We kept stopping to gaze back at the majesty of "Lonely Mountain" slowly receding to the south. Here, where there are more mountains than people, and a prominent denizen of the landscape may remain in view for several days' walk, one becomes familiar with them. First, by regarding them from some other high vantage perhaps one hundred miles distant, then coming to know them through ascent and descent of the passes between them. They provide a hammer blow struck for reality, an untarnished mirror where the subjective faces the objective without organic diversion, each attaining definition, identity and consciousness.

Boumitse-La led us through a darkening overcast into Photaksar, which I took to be (though no reliable topographical map existed at the time, and we were without benefit of an altimeter) the highest sizeable habitation which we had yet to come upon. Draped over a narrow ridge which rose between twin abysses, it didn't appear at first glance to be a place

". . . upon meeting an extremely lucid, ancient villager at day's end, this offered proof of method in their modesty."

81

where I would wish to raise children. But children it was who greeted us, and a straight talking, functional mother offered us the lodgings we sought. With the altitude, their barley was even further behind, and one could see that snow still lay in northern exposed interstices just above the village. But here again the melt-off had been tapped, and the faeces and the seed and the hoeing and the care had enabled a culture to cling to the rock. Paddy and I noted this impressive resolve, and upon meeting an extremely lucid, ancient villager at day's end, this offered proof of method in their modesty.

❋　　❋

11.

A CLUSTER OF HUMAN GRACE

Travels in Zanskar are concerned with rising and falling, mounting and plunging, soaring and sinking. What else could await us from "down" here in Photaksar but another ascent? The heavy atmospheric pall of the previous day had passed like a wave, having rendered the sky ever more cobalt. Sisir-la was one pass which we did have a reasonably reliable fix on, at fifteen thousand, six hundred odd feet. It was a relatively short climb, and confirmed for me the impression that Photaksar must be near the fourteen thousand mark. On the way up, "Lonely Mountain" appeared once again back over Boumitse-La.

We broke at the top, freeing Himself to range while we gazed. From the sunny shelter of the summit's cairn, the vacuum in our pupils drained the vista of its finest details, this breathless meeting of heaven and earth. I rooted out the camera, which was always within a great deal of whatever wadding mass was available to buffer it from the unyielding environment, and strolled over to the south side of the pass, looking to see how I might frame Lonely Mountain as horizon, when

*"I rooted out the camera ... looking to see how I might frame
Lonely Mountain as horizon, when I noticed two travellers
approaching along the path which we had just climbed."*

I noticed two travellers approaching along the path which we
had just climbed. Over several minutes they had switch-backed
their way up and joined us. One was a gently eager boy in early
teens, the other of about my own age, resplendent in a fresh
red ochre robe and a beret of brightest verdigris. Discarding
their rucksacks, the elder produced a bladder of *chang* (beer)
and partook of a lengthy draught while I studied his arresting
beret. Quenched, he offered me the *chang*, and I was grateful to sample his homebrew. Handing back the bladder, I saw
that he was quite pointedly admiring my rainbow-hued beret,
which had been crocheted by a friend in Ireland. Returning to
his pack, from deeper within he withdrew a fresh prayer flag,
which he reverently unfolded and, walking over to the cairn,
strung in amongst the array of flags which had been placed
there by other devout travellers over the years.

84

"Discarding their rucksacks, the elder produced a bladder of chang and partook of a lengthy draught while I studied his arresting beret."

"Returning to his pack, from deeper within he withdrew a fresh prayer flag, which he reverently unfolded ..."

85

For him, planning the journey would encompass the commissioning of a Lama to produce a flag to hang at each major ridge-top cairn he would encounter along his route. The wind invigorates the prayer, and its endowment manifests as blessings upon the traveller, his mission, his family and the wider world. As he cinched the tie, an eagle rose abruptly from beneath our view, and with one eye cocked in the cairn's direction, it hung there for a moment close at hand, before wheeling on one wing and rising away into the middle distance. As one we responded rapturously, and agreed that the bird had appeared with the intention of judging this most recent votive piece, contributing to a cluster of human grace which fluttered about the summit.

"As he cinched the tie, an eagle arose abruptly from beneath our view ..."

We then began a convivial and sensible game of leapfrog which was to persist for a few days. They moved along down the north side as we tarried at the summit. When, in the afternoon, we caught up to them, they served us tea. As we didn't have to set up domestics, we were able to drink and then carry on before them. And when, still later, they came upon us, we had the tea ready and they had no need of unpacking. And so it went until, after a few days, their more purposeful pace left us behind. The magnificent beret glanced back once more, and then bobbed out of sight. The night turned sharply cold, and once more we were alone on earth.

Walking and dreaming. Is there finer expression of the freedom of man than strolling out across God's earth? Or equally, enjoying untrammelled contemplation?

A'top of Gabriel the live-long night
through lidless eyes blew gales of light
swarmed galaxies streaked in exposure

Below, the waves fanned in a grid
about the sound came sailing id
the moon had been in tension

Studded stones of landscape ley
not stop the mind from disarray
I can't tell between predator or prey

within, the boundless core of light
the essence of the very night
we vowed to topple Atlas.

✸   ✸

Ever northerly, we continued to lose elevation. The vale narrowed to vertical gorge. We could have gone high, but with low water here, we stayed to the streambed. It was a chance we took. Fords were common, as cliff face blocking one bank forced us over to the other. Most were knee to thigh deep, but as we moved downstream in a new watershed, there were some deeper ones (and always the mountain swift rushing of waters). Depending on depth and current, these required some preparation. There are some things which you must keep dry. Sometimes we could all swim, other times one or another of us went to the other side, gathered a long lead to Himself, and towed him through the main current.

In one absolute sheer stretch, the local path makers had valiantly mounted a flagstone and spar catwalk climbing a hundred feet up the cliff face to avoid a savage watercourse. After scouting it to ascertain that Himself could pass, I proceeded to lead him over it. One mustn't be timid and keep too close to the inside edge: your Newtonian horse might strike his load against the rock wall and be pitched off, with or without you, in the equal opposite direction. But this too was negotiated and, beyond it, further down the canyon, we found a sizeable cave which had been scoured by high water.

One had to crawl to enter, which excluded Himself, but inside it held wonderfully cavernous acoustics, and we chose to pass a night there. Whilst still daylight we set up an abode by candlelight, and prepared food on the hissing primus. Ducking out after dark to check Himself, the soaring sable faces of our canyon created vertical horizons which revealed only a ten-degree wide swath of dense stars on a north-south axis. Ho! Ho! And once more there were the two journeymen, Jupiter and Saturn, peering into these depths, scattering sharp jeweline

"In one absolute sheer stretch, the local path makers had valiantly mounted a flagstone and spar catwalk climbing a hundred feet up the cliff face to avoid a savage watercourse."

luminescence, picked up here and there by flecks of quartz, forming constellations in the stony ground.

A morning bevy of quail scurried along the path ahead of us. After their kind, the lead male feigned a lame wing while the rest "escaped". We dropped into a lower valley, and with warmer clime, it became lush compared to what we had seen for a long time. In Honupata village a rooster crowed and I followed the disparaging clucks of his hens to the home which sold me some eggs.

On downstream, and now we were coming into Ladakh. The quality of the land, and easy access to the Indus valley, made it seem now somehow suburban. We passed a pedestrian with a pink Chinese sunshade. At Wanla we come upon the terminus of a dusty road. In Tarshit there was a school. After another day we arrived, at dusk, into Lamayuru, a foreboding fortress of a Lamasery rising out of a tumulus in silhouette, with bright Venus crowning her *gompa*.

Here we met a scent of the Indus, and we sought a fortnight's room and board for Himself, as we wished to go down to the road and catch a summer bus heading from Srinagar east to Leh. A businesslike Lama agreed to mind Himself and stow our gear during this time, and we passed a night in the Lamasery. That night we heard a curious local legend connected with Lamayuru, one which has ties with similar tales in Kashmir, and westwards. It concerns the arrival in this region of a holy man, accompanied by his mother, about two thousand years ago.

As a matter of local fact this holy man is asserted to have been Jesus. According to the story, this man had suffered greatly in his homeland, and came here where he was welcomed, and where he lived out his days. I do not know the source of these

"We passed a pedestrian with a pink Chinese sunshade."

claims, only that one hears this spoken of with great reverence in Muslim Kashmir and Buddhist Ladakh.

❋   ❋

In the cool morning three boys sat on a promontory outside the Lamasery walls, singing in and out of harmony. Their clear voices led to the valley below, below the chiselled furrowed heights, below the green of the valley floor where the sun was already scattering its blind light of day, down into the sky-blue of the river. Paddy and I, with light packs, headed off in the direction of The Road.

As we dropped down from the Lamasery we saw a group of men sitting in a circle. We could see by their dress and bearing that they were all Zanskari travellers, coming to and going from this the outside world. Sitting amongst them were our leap-frogging friends from Sisir-La, the elder with that beau-

91

tiful beret raked across his swept-back quiff. Spotting us, he greeted us profusely and invited us to join the conference. We were going to Leh. He was bound for Kargil. I asked him if he wanted to swap hats, and he jumped at it. I tried his on, and he modelled mine. "*Demoo*" can mean "cow" or, at a stretch, "beautiful". This was the only thing I could think of saying when I saw my multi-coloured beret on him. This nearly scuttled the deal, as it was evident he did not want to appear to be "*demoo*". He and I both blushed while the rest roared. The conference ended suddenly when the approaching sound of a labouring bus reached us (our first motor vehicle in nearly two months), and we made for the road to hail it. And I had acquired a new hat!

12.

EAST

It was disconcerting to encounter motor vehicles again, let alone mount one. But, gazing resignedly at each other, we recalled the advantageous leap across a landscape which their utilisation conferred, and the thought of the many miles which yawned between us and our hopes of rest and recuperation compelled us to hop aboard. An engrossing second class bus ride ensued, bearing us east up the Indus Valley to Leh, the capital city of Ladakh. Leh offered us respite and a chance to get out of the wind, and was like a holiday after our travails in Zanskar. We refreshed our ability to walk streets, eat in restaurants, meet Europeans and speak English, and had time for reflection on travels past and awaiting. And, as Leh is the leading interface between the outer world and this region, we could observe the effects of modern times upon this hitherto isolated region.

Preceding the 1962 war between India and China, the latter had "conquered" fully a third of Ladakh before it was noticed. When this fact came to India's attention, the road was built from Kashmir, up over Zoji-La, Namika-la, and Fotu-La (at the expense of hundreds of lives), following the Indus to Leh to mount Ladakh's defence. China consolidated her disputed holding and hostilities ceased, but overnight a permanent contingent of twenty thousand Indian soldiers was established outside Leh, and this was the first major impact in modern times upon local customs. The short war meant that the road, now uncluttered by military convoy, opened the gates for the real shock troops. First the traders, then the tourists and missionaries, found they had access to a pristine destination which previously had been accessible only by a walk of the best part of two hundred gruelling miles. "Progress has its price" indeed; for everything gained by this interaction, there appears to have been considerable loss, and there was certainly an amount of disquiet about the place.

The main market street of Leh, from a 1982
painting by Esther Kevin

One dispute involved a protest about a European tourist who had swatted at a child who he had maintained was "pestering" him, and this was considered quite rightfully as despicable and intolerable. "Downtown", local students were organising semi-violent demonstrations at the local Indian government administration headquarters, complaining about various unsatisfactory conditions regarding the latter's occupancy. Tibetan, Kashmiri and Indian traders were squabbling over pitches. Mixing is the nature of the age, but here one could only wonder what was going through the mind of a man whose family had been ploughing the same ground for thirty generations, when confronted with droves of people who appeared to leisure for a living.

I was attracted to, and ended up several times in the company of, young Ladakhis home from university studies in India. They offered the most comprehensive views of the changes taking place. Their reactions ranged from critical/sceptical to swept-off-their-feet seduced. English-speaking, they were great tutors of Ladakhi, proud of their language and delighted that someone wanted to grasp its rudiments. Happily there appeared to be cordial relations, or at the very least mutual tolerance, between the Indian Army personnel stationed nearby and the citizens of Leh.

The Army's volleyball league final was well attended by the locals. I was recruited into a team consisting of tourists who challenged, but were dispatched 2-1 by these champions, attracting a huge crowd which cheered on both sides equally (and where I remet the former companion from Zoji-la, who had suffered the month-long round of rabies vaccination, recovered from his dog bites and admirably persevered). But after a week, all of this urban business seemed too distracting from my own quest, and I found it hard to reconcile being part of an invasion which casually drove down streets where the use of wheels had been taboo only a few years before. So I retreated for the most part back to the little rented house in the barley fields above the city to collect my notes, sketch, write, meditate and, for circulation, take a stroll in the evening along the outer ways in the opposite direction to the lights.

> *Evening, now, and in the sun's sweep*
> *the shadows of circle-sewn grain,*
> *a mighty horizon, Kong-maru*
> *you fairly dwarf the Indus plain.*
> *tillers, millers, glacier-drinkers, all*
> *live within my eye;*
> *the centre reached, now here's a stir,*
> *the breeze of dusk sets prayer flags fly.*

✵   ✵

Paddy diligently visited most of the famous Lamaseries of the Leh vicinity, but I demurred on account of the crowds, the admission fees, and the Lama-cum-merchants. Finally, I came out of my shell and went to Phyang Lamasery, as this held the attraction of being the occasion of their *stad-mo*, or summer moon mystery play, a prospect that fascinated me. Joining up with two women (one of South American and the other of European origin) whose acquaintance I had made, a short bus ride a few miles to the west of Leh delivered us outside the large Lamasery walls. Inside, there was an enormous courtyard, the borders of which were packed to capacity, leaving the centre space for the players and their dance of elements in the

Portals to a Lamasery

round. Again, this was a Bon holdover, finding expression in a Buddhist context, played out in the afternoon sun.

We witnessed a wonderful and awe-inspiring pageant offering an allegory of life, as hideously masked dancing Lamas (as portrayed on the cover image of this book), representing the passions, hacked away at our passive protagonist, who was everyman as dough mannequin, thoughtfully stuffed with sheep's organs for effect, in a ritual which harkened back to the distant practice of human sacrifice. But, more importantly, it portrayed in dramatic fashion the all-around suffering of our incarnation in this world (the essential message of Tibetan Buddhism). Its depiction is not solely tragic – for this would miss the point – but is full of spontaneous and farcical comedy which offers some redemption.

But what is it with me? If I attend the circus I am invariably drawn out of the crowd to lend assistance to (that is, be the target for) the knife-thrower, while here, all thought of remaining anonymous in the throng disappeared as the fattest dancing Lama, who also sported the most repulsive mask, suddenly made a beeline for me and jumped into my lap and, writhing together, we collapsed in the dust. I think this was the funniest moment for the crowd. All the while, the energetic, rousing and other-worldly orchestra in the shade of the balcony would spring into a lively allegro, and then just as suddenly fall silent once more.

Cymbal rides, demon reels.
Cymbals crash, demon whorls
and circles
and the sword comes down.
Brain cells, entrails, bowels, genitals
flung about the butcher's block.
Drums of copper, oboe wails.

So much for rest and recuperation – we had had enough. I collected Lobsang Tchamchoop's watch from the watchmaker and vowed to keep it ticking until we found him again. After a final swim in the Indus at Choklamsar, we bussed back to Lamayuru with our thoughts quickening at the prospect of returning to Himself, to the trail before us, and to Zanskar.

❄   ❄

13.

To Remind Us We Were on Earth

As I entered his stable, Himself snorted, somewhat con-temptuously, but I read this as an affirmation of our bond. Regarding him, it was clear he had lost a bit of condition and had obviously not been exercised. Be that as it may, a tight packet of Paddy's small denomination rupee notes saw the Lama who had minded him squared away, but it was made clear that we were not entirely happy with his care.

We collected the rest of our gear and, though late in the day, were eager to return into the mountains. Saddling up, we left Lamayuru as we found it, with a dusky Venus hanging there to the southwest to remind us we were on earth. Southbound, well into July, we were now able to dispense with the tent many nights. South we went, through the fords of the chasms now familiar, with however the added concern of seeing Lobsang's watch safely through the rushing waters. Back over Sisir-La we returned to the majestic domain of Lonely Mountain. With Singa-la we were once more in the Zanskar catchment.

The passage of Netuksi-La saw us switch-backing down the scree to the Lingshet *gompa* where our previous warm reception was now to be exceeded most rapturously. We were met, upon our descent, with a clamorous sound of drums, wood-wind, and brass rising from below, proclaiming that their *Ngunes* (July) Summer Moon Festival was in full swing. Exuberant Lamas and children came running up the trail to greet us, full of proclamation that our arrival at this moment was most auspicious. With no more than a fetching smile as credential, a young lad secured Himself from our grasp and took him away to be tended, as we were being rush-ushered by a monk to the villager's dance below the Lamasery.

People had flocked here on foot from outlying habitations fifty miles and more away. In their finest felts, corduroys, velvets and jewellery, they were seated in a ring around the musicians and the dancers. First a men's dance, the tail of their silken waist sashes held aloft in one hand, the other placed on a hip; stepping in a circled procession, rotating this way, then the other, all movements slow and graceful, holding some distant relation to the music which, by contrast, was wildly ecstatic, reminiscent of a freeform jazz piece. Then a women's dance, with simple and elegant gestures (*mudra*), followed by men and women weaving together, all the while our cups kept to the full with *chang* of various vintages. The music, dancing and *chang* went on well into the night until the last stalwarts retired and the stars could be heard once more.

The next day, the festivities moved up into the courtyard of the *gompa*, where the Lamasery's substantial library had been brought out under a balcony for its annual airing and blessing.

Eight Lamas, seated on the clay opposite each other, chanted an invocation as dogs ran about and people began to arrive. The dances and music were repeated, though the *chang* was absent within the sacred *gompa* walls. The climax of the

The dun-chens, or great horns, set the tone for the occasion.

"First a men's dance, the tail of their silken waist sashes held aloft in one hand, the other placed on a hip."

*"Then a women's dance, with simple and elegant gestures
(mudra), followed by men and women weaving together..."*

*A balcony fills with women and children, dressed
in their finest for the event.*

*"... the Lamasery's substantial library had been brought out
under a balcony for its annual airing and blessing."*

*The books are blessed in the afternoon sun and then,
borne upon willing shoulders, carried around the perimeter
of the Lamasery's walls in an act of purification before
returning to the Library.*

afternoon came at the close of dancing. With *hareep* (oboe) wailing and drums in absolute abandon, people began shouldering the large books and circumambulating the outer walls of the *gompa* clockwise. Completing this orbit, the books were returned to the door of the main temple where they were received and replaced by waiting Lamas. Encouraged by several vociferous hosts, I bore a book about the circuit, the devout lining the route bowing to the books as the bearers passed. All tomes safely home, the multitude returned to the previous day's venue for final dances, and a taste of *chang* to slake the afternoon's thirst.

❉   ❉

14.

THAT LITTLE PIECE OF VERDANT INLAY

Confident in our knowledge of the landscape, we continued over Hanuma-la and dropped back down into that little piece of verdant inlay at Kutykit along the Omachu stream. Paddy and I had agreed on the way north that the sally coppice at Kutykit would be a good place to set up camp for several days upon our return south. We both had a yearning for still life. I wanted to break out my watercolours again, and Paddy wanted to practice his calligraphy. We achieved these pursuits in between holding court as, with mid-summer, there was now the wonderful diversion of seasonal travellers coming to use the bridge nearby: a few groups returning from the Lingshet Summer Moon Festival to the south; a horse- and yak-borne wedding troupe; random, mendicant wanderers.

On the second day, an older woman appeared from the wilds upstream, saying that some sheep had strayed and eluded her. Could she leave her young grandson with us while she searched? This was fine by us as he proved to be a delightful and self-sufficient young lad of six or seven. He watched me mix and apply colours for awhile and, tiring of this, he busied himself chiselling a mini-*chorten* with a crude tool out of an alabaster pebble. When the grandmother returned to collect him some hours later, he looked up at me and pressed it into my palm. They then became regular visitors to our camp, bringing us sheep's cheese and yak curd and staying to drink tea.

A solitary traveller joined the four of us one afternoon in the leafy shade, so Paddy poked the fire and brought the kettle back to the boil. He had a rucksack full of merchandise, some of it on order, some of his own speculation. I'd never worn a ring, but one of several on his fingers caught my eye. A mandala of various turquoises, the round centrepiece circled by eight teardrops set in black pitch amidst crudely beautiful silver craft. I inquired as to its value, then made, and had rejected, a bid. Not enough. Conversation drifted back and forth between discussing the ring's history and value, to all of the other easy concerns of a full summer's day. He fingered the last of the *tsampa* out of his bowl, thanked us, and bid us "*julay*" ("hello" and "goodbye"). Now it was my turn. I wanted the ring and had to give in. The smile must have been on his face before I hailed him. Returning, the bowl was produced once more, and we had another round of tea to savour the transaction from all sides.

✳   ✳

Several familiar monks welcomed us upon our return to the Karsha *gompa* some days later. They looked after Himself and helped us with our bags up to Lobsang Tchamchoops's apartment. Lobsang was not in, but his teacher was there in the lower flat. Without rising he nodded a greeting. He had just commenced carving the sacred characters onto another reddened stone. Not wishing to disturb him we put the primus going up on the balcony and settled into that view of views, breaking only to serve tea to the master below. During the afternoon we noticed a small cloud of dust being kicked up by a lone runner making his way across the expansive plain below. "That must be Lobsang," and over the next hour we continued to take an interest in the figure as it gradually emerged from its own dust and drew near to the village below the Lamasery. Up to and through the gates, climbing the stone-staired rise, and finally, the breathless Lobsang Tchamchoops emerged on to the balcony, exclaiming "Li Tai Po! Kai Lung!", and burst into tears. Oh! He had wondered after us, and had gathered accounts of our being sighted or met; there was now even a song and a long poem composed about us (which thankfully we never heard!).

"How were the northern passes? Were you surrounded by the wind?" I kept him company in the tiny kitchen while he prepared the *thugpa*. Then, and only then, when we had finished our meal and the light was dying, I scratched my head, said something close to "I nearly forgot", produced the watch from my breast pocket and presented it to Lobsang. He held it aloft before bringing it to his ear to hear its heart beating for the first time ever. Then again he burst into tears.

A week and more was given to filling our every pore with sonorous chant, lowliest-droned copper horn (the magnificent *dun-chen*), piercing cymbal and transcendent mountain incense in the other-worldly Karsha *gompa*. Here, waves are the key to dispassionate contemplation, where ceremonies are dedicated to the sprouting of grain by music alone. I came to see light and sound sharing a single spectrum, overlapping even, so that one could not say with authority where one ended and the other began.

The tea pot is never far from the gompa.

There was much to ponder as we were welcomed into the bosom of the Lamasery. Only the sense of the season's sun slipping south roused us from a desire to dwell within interminably, but with the days beginning to shorten, we bade farewell to Lobsang and the *gompa*. From his cell he escorted us down the steeply wending stairs. Lobsang's heart was in his face and his mind was on his sleeve. The mood progressed like a river and was easy to follow, from pool to riffle to glide. None of

*A Lama of Karsha, with the 600-year-old Bon/Buddhist
"Wheel of Life" fresco under a colonnade – left unrestored,
to remind all of imminent decay.*

us wanted to part company, so in slow motion we paused at the formidable Lamasery gate to collect Himself from the lodge. The saddle bags went on and we ambled away, waving once before the gates were closed.

With late July's long sunny days the rivers were in full spate with glacial melt-off. As fording this torrent was now out of the question, we headed upstream along the River Doda to use the bridge at Tungri. Proceeding downstream along the south bank, we dallied at the Sani *gompa* to view its art and architec-

One book I was carrying –
Foundations of Tibetan Mysticism
– aroused particular curiosity

ture. Its entrance portals sport an erect plaster phallus (the frankness of even a holy place!). This is the message – return to source! This is where we are coming from. Look at reality! Look at desire! Look at suffering! It is all so different from how we spent the last millennia, seeking solace in logic and conquest, inventing clever machines to refine genocide, land-grabbing the high moral ground to justify some grand manifest destiny. The approach here resides so many worlds away from ours that I think it is beyond our comprehension. We seek "diversion" in our lives, they abhor it. It is quite different here.

✳   ✳

15.

RETURN TO THE KINGDOM

Beyond the Sani *gompa*, an easy amble completed our return to the Kingdom. In the afternoon the three of us trod into Padum town, kicking dust up in the windless, random, mediaeval streets, and we made our way up past the chorten to keep what I had insisted to the sceptical Paddy was an appointment with the King, Tashi Nyamgal. Locating his white-washed abode, Paddy's and my harsh Tibetan, together with our illustrious pony's snorts and whinnies, must have sounded like certain Bremen musicians. The disturbance roused him, and he appeared from an upper window with a whole-hearted welcome. Bounding out into the street, and following further greetings, an exchange of news, and an expression of admiration for our horse, he firstly housed Himself with water and hay, and then kindly led us up to a comfortable second floor lodging. This, to our continuing delight, had a pleasing aspect towards the waving grain fields, and the mountains to the southwest. He then left us to ourselves to settle in, issuing, as he parted, an invitation to the evening meal. As we unpacked, Paddy, who had just encountered royalty for the first time, conceded that he had been wrong to doubt this welcome a few moons before (it is difficult to get Paddy to concede *any-thing!*), and to add that he felt very much at home.

Tashi's congenial and cosmopolitan company began to reveal itself. Related to the Kings of old Ladakh, he had been dispossessed of much of his material past by marauding *dacoits* (thieves) from beyond Kashmir many years before. But this had not discouraged his taste for human cultural variety, and he had obviously enjoyed it to the point where he hungered for it, and we were the nearest thing to "it" that he would have encountered in some time. He had travelled the world beyond (even well down into India), and this set him apart from others. Discourse, however stuttered, was welcome, and he warmed to our efforts at conversing with him in his mother's tongue. Hence he was more than patient with all of our queries. As a broker he was unparalleled in all of our travels – he encourged us to ask and ask again. As I write now, I think of all the other questions I would have put to him but was unable. And yet at times, in the breadth of his company, all was self-evident without any need to assay.

By day I followed him into his fields. Into his seventies, he nevertheless undertook his own irrigation and crop culture chores. A deft touch of the hoe here breeched a sluice, diverting a measured flood of precious water into a terrace of his now-ripening barley. Skipping across the border, another touch there staunched the bed from discharging. Pausing awhile and, seeing the furrows slaked, he then repaired the breech and allowed the source to wend away. This was a graceful agrarian dance to behold, and I was rapt. Over to the wheat garden to repeat the exercise, then a visit to his peas, which were not in need of water for the foliage, now withering, crackled between his inspecting finger and thumb, and the ripened pods were fit for harvest.

Nocturnally, the same purpose attended his inner life. A simple question about the constitution of the local calendar launched him from wistful recline into immediate action. "Come with me!", and again, only just, as I struggled to shadow him up to the penthouse. There he rolled out Zanskar's calendar, produced by his own hand. Even in these progressive times, it remained one of the *gyalpo's* (King's) duties to divide the year into literal months. In the butter-light he considered it attentively, as it was still a work in progress. Then, as we were in his study, he produced a map of the world (the only other material possession, apart from a ballpoint pen, which distinguished him as King!) and wanted to know where Ireland was and, his curiosity being without limit, how did people live there, what crops did they grow, how did they travel, and on and on into the night, with me trying to explain all of this.

Another day Tashi escorted me here and there through the hinterlands of Padum to introduce the ways of the people. On several occasions a recurring theme cropped up. Several we met suggested a resemblance between Tashi and myself, at times accompanied with a good-natured ribbing that, as Tashi had gone walkabout some thirty years previously, and I was twenty-nine, "Is this the prodigal son? Ha ha ha!" So all had a good laugh at our expense, but this only fastened a filial bond.

Inevitably, the moment arrived when Tashi had to temporarily withdraw his patronage. A stout, assured woman arrived, charging us with an offense. Not only had our horse, grazing the borders, munched a corner of her barley, but then had the audacity to cover a mare of hers which she had been "saving for a stallion she had her eye on". Paddy had to be restrained

The King and I

from insisting that stud fees might well cancel out any crop damage, but before us lay proof of irrefutable misdemeanour. Now, to follow, there was a bit of diplomacy, the observation of local protocol, and then passing of judgement. Tashi, to his credit *and* discomfort, played the "fair witness", came down in her favour, and we had to part with a few rupees. This spelled the end of the matter, though we did offer a few more rupees to provide hay for Himself until further notice.

❋   ❋

A wedding was due to arrive in Padum on the following day. Tashi invited me to come as far as Pipiting village (founded upon its extraordinary drumlin) to meet the entourage and accompany its final stages back into town. I was game, so we scampered off through the outer ways leading from Padum, a brisk sirocco rattling the barley fields under a punishing sun. We caught up with the matrimonial throng in the centre of the sacred village; a dozen horsemen escorted the bride amongst an undulating tide of well-wishers.

We had joined the party beside a *chorten* (holy place), where they had all stopped for the obligatory round of music, dancing and *chang*. A hospitable soul kept me in *arak* (distillate of *chang*) until I was well merry. Tashi, with total attention and care, shifted me here and there to get a good view of the proceedings. The escorts wore ancient split cane ceremonial hats and, trance-like, they danced through their paces. Suddenly, they all mounted and rode like thunder another few hundred yards to the next holy place and, as the pedestrians caught up, the round was repeated.

At length, the King and I broke from this to return to his house for the evening *tsampa*. As night fell, one could make out the silhouettes of the mounted horses galloping along the trail through the barley fields, their masters half-crazed with the day, and the heavy bronze bells about the horses' necks sounding a mad cacophony of gongs. Having eaten, we returned to the pageant. One rider carried drums between his legs, and he was pounding away as his horse raced along, favouring his drumsticks to the reins, in sharp contrast to the grip one imagined the abstemious bride had upon her driver. After dark fell we joined the final ceremony of marriage and blessing of the dowry, enacted by a shamanistic Lama in the throes of a wild dance amidst the bonfires.

✻   ✻

I slept into the morning and, rousing, drank a lot of water to clear my head and then slipped down the town towards the outer ways where the intriguingly blue River Tsarap emerged from its mysterious valley to the southeast. I met few and sought fewer, wishing to focus on the verses forming in my head. I was in labour over a poem, and struggling to see if I could bring it to life in Tibetan. I returned to precipitating tea which cleared my thoughts. With purpose, I returned to my chambers, fetched my stylus and struggled to utter what I might discover. As the final afternoon became the final evening, and as the landscape through the large window became a negative of itself with nightfall, Tashi called to our quarters, seated himself and, without reversion to other discourse, I recited the poem which I had composed for him:

> *E nyamo nya stot*
> *jikstom nyis.*
> *Chig: sa, chu, meay, lung, nam....*
> *semcha spos.*
> *Nyi, od thong-ba,*
> *spos met.*
> *Taksa, dul, dulches,*
> *ston, yar, speet, gun chet:*
> *E lam caru labanok?*

The height of my poetic powers! Simple Tibetan, employing the profundity of the local world to offer two contrasting themes, resolving them with a question, after the local fashion. Translating:

This morning I see
two worlds.
The one, of water, earth, fire, air, aether,
A dance of change.
The other, of hollow light,
unchanging.
Now to walk; walking, through
spring, summer, autumn, winter.
To where does this way lead?

We sat in silence for some time, both gazing from the dark room out into a nocturnally becalmed landscape. The quarter moon had cleared a lofty saddle to the south and now illuminated the barley. The shadows spawned thereby crept along in a slow arc. Tashi hummed a sigh, and expressed appreciation at the effort.

Thinking broadly, I do not believe that population pressures forced people such as these to live in apparent, relative desolation. A far-sighted view of human purpose can, in a culture such as this, find a way to improve the chances of fostering true human nobility. As this virtue is often in inverse proportion to the degree of material splendour attained, a society may choose to set boundaries upon the material potential of their lives. Consider the Zanskaris, Hopis, Quakers and Shakers.

Here, it is as if a landscape, a climate, was able to produce a sensible centre-point for human behaviour. This is difficult to convey to our "best of all possible worlds", where many might conclude that our subjects here must be considered impoverished. But to clarify: these people aren't Puritans, and most certainly are not wasting time trying to deny their lusty nature. No, people *live* here, eating and drinking and making themselves beautiful, laughing and crying and getting angry and love-making to the hilt. But the capacity to generate wealth is limited, and so with it the seeming concomitant alienation.

An optimum blend of necessary material and spiritual concerns pertains. An easy, natural discipline – and a permanent relationship with the earth – provide the keel and rudder for this course. No one here appeared unhoused or unfed, or cast adrift without spiritual sustenance. In contrast, the frenzy of our genetic hangover, craving achievement, blinds one to life's meaning. This leisure which has been attained in the "modern world" leaves one prepared for little else than to go on building up material inventories (shopping). Compared with these serious attempts at conscious living, we are a youthful, rabid and dangerous breed for whom there is no collective cure other than to run the course. Does wisdom ever arise, spontaneously, without first folly?

Before entering these mountains, Paddy and I had discussed the likely fragility of the status quo, and the ability of the banal, telecommunicating, commercial juggernaut (of which we were unwitting emissaries) to destabilise the hard-won integrity of such a society. After weighing and rejecting the notion of not travelling there at all, we agreed 1) to travel as simply as possible (and not carry any flash gear); 2) to do our utmost to acquire and respect the native tongue in our communications; and 3), to ensure that we have the greatest regard for local custom. The concern, since justified, was for a culture so old and remote that its origins, its *raison d'être*, somehow half forgotten over the centuries, would be open to seduction by the very forces it fled.

I don't agree much with Mao, but I think this may be what he meant when he wrote of "perpetual revolution", where a degree of self-imposed struggle, combined with a strong memory of previous, insufficient conditions, keeps one on the straight and narrow. Otherwise, the wits go dull, the sense of justice and compassion within the community are gradually eroded, and people retreat into a narrow and indifferent cellular comfort. Or they go where the lights seem to be bright, in the hope that they will at least find their consuming diversions well illuminated.

✳   ✳

16.

THE RIVER TSARAP

We traipsed off southeast into the River Tsarap valley one morning, pausing at the last to look back once more at Padum. From Padum we were to follow the Tsarap upstream for a few days, then veer off to climb Shingo-la over the main Himalayas, and down into India. Wistfully, we sensed the journey's end, and our pace was slack. For the time being, however, we were still in Zanskar, and we delighted at the new landscape of this valley. Whereas the Doda had been brown, turbid and muddied, the Tsarap was blue and singing through meandering rapids, the valley full of morning sunshine.

We walked as far as Mune village, and were encouraged to set up our camp in the porch of the tiny *gompa*. The entire village joined us as we prepared the evening meal. They sat in rows radiating out from our improvised quarters and, as we cooked and ate, there was an ongoing exchange of banter. With dusk people began drifting away, but a young woman of extraordinary beauty stayed behind and approached me to draw attention to a deep festering burn she had received to her arm. I got out my herbals, made up a poultice of golden seal to draw the poison, and then applied comfrey cream (for want of anything else) around the affected area. She was bashful and, thanking me awkwardly, bade me goodnight.

In the morning two curious things happened. First, Himself had disappeared from the end of an unslippable tether and, with the aid of some nods and winks from sympathetic villagers, we traced him to where he was tied up in a stall. An older woman had taken a fancy to him and stolen him! We were assured that this was normal behaviour for her, and that we should not take any notice! The second thing was that the young woman with the burn came back to visit, all smiles. She turned up her sleeve to reveal that, overnight, it had miraculously healed almost completely. We were all astounded, and I had to marvel at the role of faith in healing. As Alexandra David-Neel noted on her early Tibetan sojourns, "*Mos gus yod na khyi so od tung*" ("If there is veneration, even a dog's tooth emits light").

Our possessions gathered, a half-day's amble (our "constitutional", says Paddy) upstream from Mune led to the meeting and, for us, the parting, of the Tsarap and Kargya Rivers. We crossed a bridge over the latter which spanned a deep narrows, and sought lodging at an expansive residence which acted as a formal roadhouse. Its aspect provided the place name of Puhni with more hours of direct sunlight than the steep valley from which we had emerged, and there was a leafy response to the mini-climate thus afforded. Our host was a rotund, friendly, generous man who couldn't do enough to make sure we were content; hence we delighted in unburdening our loads, savouring his fare, and wandering along his outer ways. He even agreed to look after Himself for the following day (for he clearly admired him), and this would release us for a lightly-equipped stroll up the northeast canyon to visit Fuktal, the southern-most Lamasery of Zanskar. We thanked him for this and welcomed the chance to undertake a final daytrip in the course of our strange and sustained pilgrimage.

After a lie-in, we awoke, and enjoyed a languorous breakfast of barley gruel and endless tea. Mid-morning was considered to be early enough for departure upon what had been depicted as an easy ramble. Our new friend graciously accompanied us through his watered gardens, telling us to forget our horse for the day (he was a husbandman – were there plans afoot)? Little did we care if he made the most of the appearance of our valiant stallion, gesturing to us to only follow the yellow brick road which led beyond the reach of his garden. Before disappearing beyond the final coppice we waved and headed upstream.

Holding to the south bank of the River Tsarap, we made steady progress. Tame ravens landed at our feet and hopped along in front of us as we held to the impeccably maintained path. At last we came to the audacious bridge which had precluded Himself accompanying us. In effect, it was a woven wicker basket slung perhaps sixty feet across the torrent, with what must have been a ton of flagstones laid along it. By now we possessed a given faith in these structures, and we strode right down and crossed it.

Over a small ford, around a few more bends, and imposing Fuktal Lamasery came into view. Its presence suggests the lines along which a Lamasery develops as an institution. High in the cliff face is set an enormous cave, hollowed, perhaps, by the river's course in an earlier epoch. A holy man, in his commitment to enlightenment, comes here for years of solitary contemplation. His reputation carries afar and, following persistent entreaty, he agrees to act as mentor to a student or two. The saint passes on, and the cave becomes a place of pilgrimage. Some are called, and remain to study with his disciples.

*"At last we came to the audacious bridge which had precluded
Himself accompanying us."*

The cave becomes crowded, so a shelter, and then two more,
spring up. Progressively, over generations, more seekers arrive,
a *gompa* is consecrated, and the spill-over of support buildings
appears along down the cliff face. Fuktal has a resident population of three hundred Lamas, though, with most now at traditional late summer travels, we found it nearly deserted.

The first person we met was one of the Lamasery's cooks.
Following the cook to the kitchen, he boiled the kettle, made
tea, vigorously churned the butter and the tea together, reheated the consommé-like brew, and then served it with a small
bag of roast *tsampa*. If Dickens had been Tibetan he would
have chronicled this kitchen. The roof stopped short of joining
with the vertical face of the rear wall of bedrock. Fires were
kindled against this, establishing a chimney effect which draft-
ed most of the smoke away. Culinary equipment was similar
to any kitchen here, but was on an enormous scale to cater for

Around a few bends, imposing Fuktal came into view.

the large Lama population, and there was an array of cranes and gantries in support to shift pots, pans and kettles on and off the fire. Rock and roof beams alike glistened a shiny black from the centuries of evaporated butter and tars from the fire which had seeped into them. One could imagine the bustle and atmosphere of the kitchen in full swing.

After several servings of tea another Lama wandered in. Greeting us, he helped himself to tea and sat down. He was intensely curious about us and watched us closely as we answered his queries. His affable, direct manner prompted me to press him for his opinion on a few matters, including the desecration of Tibet, and what he thought of the presence of the likes of Paddy and myself? He condemned the loss of life and sacred property, but was unsentimental towards Tibet, and Lhasa-as-institution.

"Entities come into being, live out their lives, and transmutate. Why should it be different with Tibet?" As for us, he had travelled himself, and understood our presence. "It is a time of flowering and seeding, and a time of great change," was his worldly pronouncement. Zanskar would change drastically in years to come, but neither Tibet nor Zanskar would die. How could anything truly die? It would be carried off, as seeds, "on the wind, in your hearts," then laughing, "and probably in your rucksacks."

"Come," he beckoned, and led us up into the cave. In the shadowed reaches there was an exquisite shrine to the Enlightened One. A spring bubbled up out of the floor, setting an appropriate melody for the all-pervading sense of peace within Fuktal's sacred grotto.

❄   ❄

17.

HIMALAYA

The following night we camped above Kargya, and from there the next morning we commenced our final climb, up the Shingo-la ("Pass of no wood/vegetation"). Once more the way was unclear, for the elements forbade any semblance of a path. But we reckoned with the sun, and the orientation of the ridges above and, after due consideration, simply had to presume that we were on the right way. There was much fording back and forth across the thankfully shallow upland sources of the River Tsarap. As we rose, however, it became clear that this massif was of a different nature from any before – broader, bolder, with much evidence of higher rain and snowfall.

We had been dealing with the arid Zanskar and Ladakhi mountain ranges to the north, where there is more ice than snow, and this was now the Himalaya that we were traversing. The stones quickly gave way to a blindingly white world of freshly-fallen snow. At first it was wet and slushy, but over a sharp climb of an hour or more it became thick ice underfoot. We squinted our way through a brief but lusty storm which blew through, bringing a fresh layer to the glazing. It cleared as we gained the summit. Looking back to the north from this lofty watershed, we imagined this ice melting, trickling down into a Tsarap tributary, flowing through Mune and Pune villages, meandering past Padum and, not before irrigating the King's fields, joining the Doda waters to become the River Zanskar. And we thought of Zanskar, and all of our experiences, and we knew we had been blessed to witness that world. Now, to the south, before and below us, lay the sultry subcontinent under the late monsoon. I wanted to stay awhile beside the prayer flags, breathing deeply, as if I would not be able to come up for air again for a long time. A single step in descent meant we had left old Tibet.

Then we were in India. Dropping some miles down the south face, we dipped below the snowline before meeting a Hindu goatherd under a gaily-coloured woollen hat minding his forty charges.

"Namaste" ("God residing in me respects God residing in you") came his greeting, and he bore tidings: the river at the bottom of the pass was unable to be forded due to water levels being driven to unheard-of heights by unprecedented snow-melt, and a large camp had been established by those who had been stranded for a few weeks now.

"Was there any way across higher up this way?"

"Usually, but the warm season had melted an old arched ice-bridge, and one would just have to wait for a few cloudy days to ease the melt-off at the confluence below."

We camped for the night, not seriously troubled by this news as we had come up against many obstacles in the course of our travels.

Knowing that the best chance to cross an unruly stream is at dawn before the rising sun goads the flow, we struck our camp while still starlit and pieced our way down the trail. First light indeed revealed a camp of more than a hundred travellers of all races and persuasions, with tents and shelters of all description pitched upon the spit thrown up by the meeting of the two rivers.

Paddy and I sized up the situation. A word with a few souls indicated that they were resigned to waiting out the high water. While we were talking, their reasoning was justified by a commotion which broke out beside the greater river. The large numbers of horses contained in the small space were restless and hungry, and a couple of them had ventured out into the current, perhaps sensing the ungrazed far shore. A poor foal had followed them and, out of its depth, was struggling to regain the strand. To no avail, as the torrent dragged him along and, as it picked up speed, sucked him under and he disappeared.

In contrast to their reaction, ours was a redoubling to not get stuck there. Handing the reins to a willing fellow, Paddy and I took a quick look upstream along the tributary, and found a swift deep narrows caused by a sheer rock face on our side. From a ledge we pitched stones towards the other side to divine the depth in slightly calmer water at what we judged to be a point we could jump to. With the water rising, we quickly hatched a plan and flipped a coin to establish our roles.

It fell for Paddy to accelerate over the four steps which the ledge afforded, and leap out over the cascade. He landed in waist-deep water and scrambled up out of it. Then, one by one, I cast our packs and bags across to him, and he secured them well up out of the river bed. I ran back down to Himself, and strung together all of the available rope we had and tied one end to his halter. When I had coiled the rest I let it fly, and at the second attempt it reached Paddy about twenty yards across what we had judged to be the least turbulent stretch. As he dug in and planted himself, I drove the horse out into the river. Now it was all up to the two of them.

Himself trotted out until he buoyed, and then swam as he swung downstream in an arc, while Paddy tugged with all of the strength he could summon. I couldn't breathe until I saw that Himself had gained his footing once more, and he rose up out of the water on the far side. I ran back up to the narrows. The half hour it had taken us to complete this exercise had seen the river rise another two feet, and widen. I stuffed my prized beret into my pocket, took my four steps, and sailed out over the deafening roar.

Landing in water which was now thundering along at shoulder depth, I used my momentum to launch into a mad stroking for the shore. Paddy was waiting with an outstretched arm. Above the din, his roaring exhortations ran into well-chosen felicitations as I collapsed upon the bank. The river had been glacier only hours before and possessed a penetrating chill. Soaked through in the morning frost, I knew I had to get moving to generate some heat in my numbing bones. We grabbed Himself and, with a wave to the incredulous throng on the other side, the three of us jogged off, not stopping until we swung around the shadows and into the glorious sunshine of the new day.

※   ※

EPILOGUE

For the record: we carried on to Darcha to the head of the road. Word spread that we had come from Zanskar and, as there were tourists gathered there, requests arose to guide them back into those mountains for a fee. With my fresh knowledge, I toyed with this notion, as there were some weeks remaining before the return of the serious snows. But I could not reconcile reappearing in that land as other than I had – feeling easy, spontaneous and genuine, all of my relations (whether with earth or people) having arisen naturally. So this constituted my advice to those who tried to persuade me to lead them into that world: if the desire is really there, find your own way.

Himself, in great condition, found a new owner and fetched a good price. I recall him with gratitude. After a spell collecting my notes and relaxing in a smart bungalow in an orchard above Manali, we visited Dharamsala to avail of the Dalai Lama's excellent library and to fraternise with his retainers. From Dharamsala, Paddy went "further east". I returned to Ireland via Bombay and London, to my children, my land, my garden, and my life.

Zanskar continued to "open up", and I understand it is now a fashionable destination. Word from that world reached me in the early 1990s: the King, Gyalpo Tashi Nyamgal, had died. Lobsang Tchamchoops had left the Lamasery and married! I don't know if his watch is still ticking.

My travels in Zanskar have continued to inform my vision and practice, and my appreciation for life. For this and for the ease with which we were welcomed in the course of our travels, I am eternally grateful to the people of Zanskar.

"Nima gyalyung tokpo chunmo duk!"

✳   ✳

Appendix A

The Zanskar Way of Life

I am aware that proper diarists seamlessly weave practical details and observations into their narrative. I have attempted to incorporate as much of this as was possible into the preceding travelogue, yet there is so much more that it may have been straining a point, or my literary abilities, to effortlessly incorporate all of this within the body text, not to mention the distinct possibility that a portion of readers may have found such a rendering cumbersome. These matters, however, are so integral to, and so telling of, life in Zanskar, that I wish to devote a section of this record to elaborate upon them. I know that there are strengths and weaknesses to my observations. An earlier fluency in the language may have augmented the gathering of data – this was not to be. But I include this Appendix as a codicil to the travelogue, with a belief that there will be some readers who will find this information of interest.

Two further considerations, moreover, compel me to develop a fuller account of life in Zanskar: firstly, that this way has now (many years on from the expedition), in the face of progress, been largely abandoned, and therefore is worth recording for posterity (as it has historical value), and secondly, that a telling of the wondrously finite number of elements in this

133

other-world may offer reminder to all as to how simple and direct life may have been, before our industrial elaborations, apart from achieving some spectacular technical tricks, took us so far from source that our focus now founders.

Hence, though no foe of Darwin, I possess this *a priori*, perhaps more cosmological, theory of evolution (more Telhard de Chardin-esque), which ignores questions of missing links. It relates rather to larger pictures, like generation of galaxies, birth of stars and through to the cooling of planetary bodies which may or may not evolve environments suitable to life as we know it. If, haply, life does emerge, it follows upon a rough mineral/ vegetable/animal route which at some point (apparently) realises self-conscious, dreaming, scheming, tool-making and club-wielding beings such as ourselves.

Concurrent with this development is the emergence of the disciplines: religion, art, astronomy/astrology, agriculture, cuisine, architecture, social structure, music, theatre, literature, physics, technology, law, metallurgy, meteorology, medicine and so on. Unlike our own age, when each of these fields are viewed as separate and requiring particular specialists, there exists an age where the boundaries are ill-defined, in fact where the several sciences are as one. If I wish to relate documentary details of life in Zanskar, it cannot proceed without this preface, as here art, religion and science reside in the same place, with very few decisions or actions taken without reference to everything else by a population of lucid polymaths. If I speak of one thing, and not another, then bearing this preface in mind, I will make my way through a sustenance/shelter/ social structure/higher-thought progression (with snippets of culinary reference scattered throughout) to the very best of my abilities.

METEOROLOGY, WATER, AGRICULTURE

Crop culture takes place only in the main valleys, which lie between eight and fourteen thousand feet. Without exception, steep mountains rise all about the valleys. There is negligible annual rain and snowfall in the valleys; indeed, they are virtual deserts (two to four inches total precipitation annually). It is for the heights to harvest the remnants of storms blown up out of the Arabian Sea or the Bay of Bengal, fully one thousand, five hundred miles away, and already well milked by half a considerable continent to the south. Falling as snow at sixteen to twenty-three thousand feet, forming glaciers which exist within larger weather cycles which see successive centuries accumulate more snowfall in winter than snowmelt in summer. Some here say that the glaciers are shrinking these last three hundred years. They no doubt have their own ebb and flow in relation to global weather, yet I am apprehensive as to how the rest of the world's consumption influences these extraordinary convex bodies of water. (I read this today, in the age of recognition of "Global Warming", and shudder. I recently read in *The Irish Times* that some Himalayan glaciers are shrinking in length by "fifteen meters per year"! If this trend continues, it would spell the end of the region's ability to support life).

The glaciers must be seen as the batteries which enable this people and culture to exist here. In deep winter all water is silent. But as the days lengthen the chorus of watercourses all begin to sing their own range of notes, until in summer, one witnesses the peculiar phenomenon of having the streams in spate during the bluest skies (when the sun melts the glaciers), while overcast weather, with spent, impotent clouds, brings low water. Habitation, and agriculture, occurs where a tributary joins the main valley, as the gravity-fed sluices tapping these streams enable an irrigation regime which delivers water to the terraced fields. Drinking water must come from artesian wells, as the mountain stream water is laced with harmful suspended scree (as ground glass to human entrails). However these tapped tributaries are the sole source of water sufficient for grain production. Their importance is summed up in the common and cheerful greeting amongst Zanskaris, "*Nyima gyalyung tokpo chunmo duk*", which translates, "As the sun shines the streams come flowing", all in agreement that this is a fine day for barley, beast or brethren. I needn't add that one employs this as a greeting even in the most appalling weather, or indeed, at nighttime.

The irrigation systems themselves are marvels of engineering: sturdy aqueducts, sometimes more than a mile in length to tap a tributary high enough to supply sufficient head, wend their way along narrow canyon walls, supported by impressive stone works. Smaller sluices branch off from these, working their way along field borders. Hoes are used to deftly divert water from these rivulets to gently quench the crop, ever mindful of eroding the precious soil.

DUNG AND PLOUGH, GRAIN AND PULSE, PASTA AND BEER

As animal dung serves as the primary fuel source, human manure (applied in the spring to assist in melting snow and thawing ground for ploughing) supplies the nutrients for soil building and crop growth. Power for ploughing is provided by the reliable and versatile yaks. These shaggy, determined little cows pull carved hardwood ploughs (usually of walnut or apricot timber imported from Ladakh or Kashmir) through the treasured topsoil.

In early June, sowing of the staples (barley, wheat and peas) is completed in the main valleys. No thoughtless broadcast, this. As the farmer seeds, a necessary trio attend comprised of a Lama, a drummer and an oboist. As the Lama chants and chimes, the drums roll in and out as nearby thunder, while the haunting oboe skirts the dry wind. Thus the seed, as it hits the ground, is blessed and energised, indeed *tuned* for germination.

A short growing season finds compensation in the high levels of ultraviolet radiation at these altitudes which hastens the crop along. Barley and wheat can be seen to go from seeding to harvest inside seven weeks!

Thrashing and winnowing take place on specially prepared smooth clay areas in plazas between houses, whereupon the barley goes into the granary for another long winter. Straw is put to many uses. With willow twigs it puts the wattle in wattle and daub, is used as reinforcement in sun-baked brick making and, as ever, as animal bedding and feed. Barley, wheat and peas are rendered into flour by water-powered mills, though one must have enough ground to get through the long freezes during winter when the mills are stopped. The barley and peas, in varying proportions the ingredients of the *tsampa* diet, are sometimes lightly roasted in broad, shallow copper pans (so shaped and constituted to achieve the best efficiency from the small fire necessitated by scant fuel) before grinding. This can be done to modify the moisture content of the corns to ease the milling, or to impart a fuller, slightly smoked flavour to the finished *tsampa*.

The mills, or *rantoks*, which yield the staple flours, warrant description. An aqueduct carries water to a carved out log headrace, which, directed underneath the mill floor, delivers it upon tuned paddles that protrude from a lump of a wooden hub, tapering above and below as a shaft. The lower millstone is fixed to the mill floor. The shaft passes through this and is keyed into the upper, rotating stone, all of this resting upon a stone bearing at the bottom end of the shaft. A conical daubed wicker basket, suspended from the low ceiling, contains the whole grain or legume. When a carved funnel is agitated by the movement of the upper stone, the grain issues forth, spilling into the central orifice and discharged as flour about the stones, whence it is gathered into small knit bags to be at the ready in capacious sleeves when tea is served. Occasionally

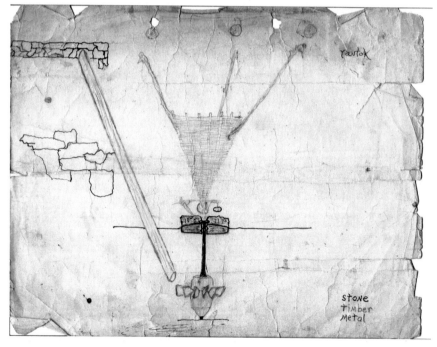

Mill schemata: "Barley, wheat, and peas are rendered as required into flour by clever water-powered mills ..."

A Lama with his bag of flour outside a low-ceilinged mill house

there are batteries of these mills in file, each reusing the water from the one above.

Thugpa is wheat flour rolled and cut into pasta strips, and generally served in a broth with any available greens, such as fresh peas or *kumuk*, the leafy green which seemingly self-seeds wherever some rare organic basis accrues.

A further use of the barley is in the making of the beer, or *chang,* which one encounters upon the same occasions as in our own lives, such as at weddings, festivals, perhaps a vessel with a meal or a sup at the end of the day. Yarrow takes the place of hops, the fermented opaque stock sometimes carelessly strained through torn muslin so that as one relaxes it may suddenly be realised that, tipsily, not alone are you drinking but indeed eating as you chew a bloated bit of grain which has slipped through the screening and into the brew. Nevertheless, it achieves the desired effect, though one can never account and say, "Three pints drunk, that's enough now" as no sooner does one take a sip or two from one's vessel when some cheery soul tops it back to the brim from a squeezed bladder.

GRASSES

Grasses as we know them do not appear in Zanskar; one finds no fescue, rye or clovers. Though it is not given dedicated fields, alfalfa (or lucerne) however, is cultivated along the sluice borders, where the ground holds enough of the passing moisture to sustain its growth. I was unable to discover its origins but it seemed to have been cultivated since time immemorial. As it is native to the Middle East (Persia/Mesopotamia) it would have easily passed this way over the centuries, and its value as animal fodder would have been immediately appreciated. Beyond that, alfalfa is a proven soil builder and, being leguminous, assists in fixing nitrogen in the thin layer of humus. I witnessed it growing upwards to a foot and a half and, upon maturity, it was cut and quickly but carefully cured in the wind and sun – the parched nature of the place would render it as dust if neglected – and this is the nourishing hay of Zanskar. We had Himself often carrying a small improvised bale of it upon his back to sustain him when we were above vegetation.

DOMESTICATED ANIMALS

Looking at livestock, any of the beasts here may be milked, shorn, or ridden etc. at a moment's notice. It goes with the patch as, given the minimalist landscape, all resources must be adaptable to several employments. The yak however is the most bountiful of all, if only for her yield of butter, hence she is "more equal" than the horse, donkey, sheep and goats. Moreover, it falls for her, or her castrated brother, to pull the plough in springtime, the low centre of gravity and compact power ideal to the conditions. She populates caravans, which appear as long black articulated snakes undulating over the landscape, bearing loads of salt or bundles of pashmina, or on her own in the company of a solitary herdsman, all but concealed under a load of firewood fetched from three days' walk away. Wedding marches often feature one of the more reliably tempered yaks carrying the drummer, his twin bongos lashed either side of her neck, the percussionist's legs like vices upon her flanks as he thunders away, favouring the slap upon his bongos to a grip upon her reins. She is shorn, her quantum length coat (in response to altitude and degree of winter) finding its way into felting and weaving, and which the women lovingly braid into each other's already substantial black tresses.

I have alluded to the horses; you have read that one became very dear to our hearts. It must have been an arduous task over generations to establish Zanskar's stable, as horses can be notoriously altitude- and climate-specific. If your travels take you over seventeen thousand feet, you would do well not to acquire one until at least ten thousand. But, like the yak, they live on little or nothing. And like the yak, these ponies are wonderfully fecund and may be successfully bred with but a wink in her direction. As to their masters, it must be their Buddhist compassion which allows them into the mind of their horses, soliciting an uncanny responsiveness – yet again, the evidence of an utter care and respect for all sentient beings.

Donkeys are for short-haul burdens about the hamlet. It is for them to bring the clay and water to the building site, and the corn to the mill. They too have their honoured place within the family. The Tibetan for donkey is *boom-poo*.

As with the Chinese, sheep and goats are the one animal, and they appear together in herds. Either may be milked for itself or for producing small quantities of cheese. They make their contribution to fuel supplies, small children following them around the day long, collecting their droppings into woven salix baskets suspended upon their backs to bring home and, when mixed and pounded with other dung in solution, produces a turf-like fuel. The wool they yield is spun, warped and woven into a range of grades for applications from sacks to trousers, or felted and dyed for hat, shoe and mattress making.

At such altitudes there seems to be some dispensation from the usual Buddhist taboo upon consumption of meat, for both lamb and goat are slaughtered, the flesh being hung to dry and cure in the parched atmosphere. This jerky, thus preserved, is soaked and boiled in the *thugpa* (pure wheat flour pasta) soup to not alone contribute sustenance to the dish but render the parched and stringy flesh edible. Make no mistake: whenever I encountered this preparation it was vitally welcome and I found myself offering profuse thanks for its appearance. Addressing the wider consumption of meat, I presumed that it was perhaps in deference to their Hindu neighbours that the sacred yak is not eaten, though I did not learn as to what end their carcasses met.

I only ever saw chickens (*jchamo*) in Northernmost Zanskar, towards the Indus valley at much lower elevation. By then an egg (*go-nya*) was a rare dinner. Two of them beaten into a *kumuk* (the common, wild, leafy green) and garlic (borne over two months from Kashmir) omelette highlighted a celebratory meal for Paddy and I, which was occasioned by *chang* and deep discussion over which came first, the *jchamo* or the *go-nya*?

DAIRY

With wheat and peas in close support, dairy produce, together with barley, form the two main staples of this region. But firstly allow the local lactose lexicon to trip off your tongue (keeping accents on the second syllable, where applicable, and a some-what less-than-Mediterranean roll upon the "*r*"'s):

Milk = *oma*

Whey = *tara*

Yoghurt = *jzo*

Cheese = *chura*

Butter = *mar*

The butter (*mar*), ah the butter. It must be mentioned in a separate breath because of the central role it has within the culture. There are no fences in Zanskar. If stock are near a ham-let and its verdant mantle of summer fields, there will be herd-boys and -girls minding them in shifts, ceaselessly by night and day, to prevent them from straying into ripening barley. One rarely sees a yak in the valley during summer, however. Largely they are taken to high altitude grazing, twelve to fifteen thou-sand feet, where they are driven between temporary camps. The camps are set up to accommodate by night a herd of up to seventy yaks within a low stone-walled corral, each yak secured to a heavy stone by a thong through its nose-ring. The beasts are individually owned but cooperatively herded. At any giv-en time, seven or eight men tending them lodge in small dark stone hovels, always one or two awake through the night with an eye out for wolves or bears. The summer is passed driving the yaks off at dawn in a different direction each day, until the time comes to shift camp. The men know their vertical prai-rie and its relative concentrations of low scrub. They also know that they will need to graze it next year, hence they are cautious not to overgraze and do damage. And, they know that energy expended in the herd roaming too far through an outrageous landscape is energy removed from milk production. The corral is auspiciously placed as the hub of this stay, and it is here where the milking takes place and the butter- and yoghurt-making arts are practised. A wizard of a churn makes the butter come.

Butterfat content of the milk is visible; I would have to estimate it in excess of 7%. As it is gathered from the churn it is salted to varying degrees, then a kilo or more is patted into (*yak*) bladders which are stitched up tight with (*yak*) gut and put in secure storage. The remaining milk is cultured to curdle,

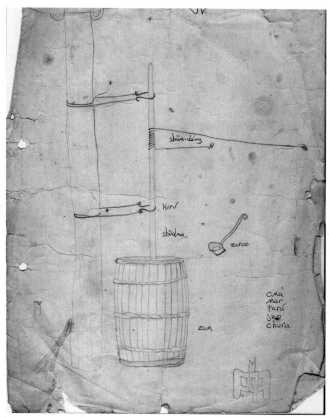

"A wizard of a churn makes the butter come..."

yielding its luscious *jzo* (yoghurt) and the prized whey (*tara*), both of which, beyond camp requirements and having short "shelf-life", are dispatched every few days back to the home village. The butter rests and matures. A portion will be given to the Lamasery associated with the area, the remainder distributed amongst the villagers for their culinary use and, if needs be, as valuable barter. Some vintage bladdersfull are put away for ten, fifty, three hundred years awaiting special occasions. One way or the other, by far the greater share ends up in the salted, buttered tea (*cha*) which is drunk in copious amounts (perhaps seven to eight cups each at regular sittings) throughout each day all through the year.

The tea-making ritual involves an elaborate procedure which is observed with little variation. Water, when boiled in a copper to brass kettle over the kippen and dung embers, receives a knowing handful of green twig tea, like a Japanese *bancha,* followed by a generous dash of salt and a measure of butter. As this emulsion is sufficiently steeped, it is sieved (always the same sieve, to recover the coagulated butter from the previous brew) into a plunger-churn and vigorously agitated to impose some degree of alchemical homogeneity upon it before it is reheated in the kettle and served. It yields a satisfying brew which has been shaped by the harsh, demanding and particular *terroir.*

Butter is furthermore employed as lubricant in mills and prayer wheels. It acts as the binder in ecclesiastic barley sculpture and, together with barley, becomes the focus of Lamaist consecration, the veritable host to the transcendent chant and the sacred gong. But stay, there is more, for on the altar behind the gong, or in an abode under the stars, there are lamps to illuminate the sacred image or the sleeping child. Butter as light!

VEGETABLES AND FRUIT

Vegetables are not cultivated *per se*. It may be due to the elevation, the short growing season, and the constant danger of frost even during the summer. Yet I was surprised not to find at least a scallion, a dwarf cabbage or something, as they are, given the extremities, most avid farmers. Perhaps this was all down to the inability to see anything through to maturity and therefore secure seeds for the following year. The one exception was peas, which are primarily grown for drying. I did have a few tastes of fresh green pod and all, and they were very welcome upon these rare occasions. But the vast majority of the peas end up being dried and ground as flour for blending in various amounts with barley meal to appear as *tsampa*. For dietary greens they fall back on a few hardy plants which are acclimatised to the harsh environment, such as the *kumuk* or Famine Weed as it is called in Ireland, which appears in stews with goat or mutton jerky and fresh wheat pasta as a welcome evening meal.

Furthermore, and for the same reasons, there is no indigenous fruit cultivation, apart from one fresh, rotund mulberry (*tschatoot*) which I discovered in the course of these travels, though I am sworn not to reveal its whereabouts. Exploring a Lamasery, I came across a quizzical stone enclosure, five feet in diameter, just taller than a man, with walls a stone or two thick. Curiosity compelled me to find the one foothold in the fragile structure which would enable me to peer over the top. As I spied a mulberry bush bearing the single fruit, there was nervous laughter behind me. Jumping back down and greeting him, the Lama politely explained that yes it was the only fruit in all the world and yes it would ripen within hours and yes would I care to join him then in dismantling the wall and partaking of the crop? What would you have done?

But this displayed the true plantsman's commitment to securing even the single fruit for the season. The stone structure, apart from keeping the mulberry bush from the almost ceaseless parching winds, would act as a thermal mass to cancel out the nightly frost from within its confines (and, hopefully, deter the would-be pilferer). I could only bow before this dedication.

FIRE

Traditionally kindled by sparks produced by flints and kippens, or the friction of heated mortar and pestle, sulphur matches had made inroads by the time we travelled to Zanskar. The dung fuel, comprised of a myriad of droppings each of which is fastidiously collected from the extensive landscape, blended with water and dried in the sun to produce a circular briquette, is wonderful for inertial heat and preserved embers, much like the Irish peat, with even a scant residual of this remaining from a given dinner fire to glow all night, ready to effortlessly rekindle the first kettle-boiling fire upon the following morning. This is supplemented by the rarer twig (even harder-won and gathered from afar) which provides the especial gastronomic or aesthetic flare to seal a dish or an occasion.

SHELTER, ARCHITECTURE, WASTE MANAGEMENT

Shelter is strong, sensible and usually quite spacious, though the degree of these qualities is generally a reflection of the altitude and therefore the relative prosperity of local agriculture, as surplus produce (achieved more easily with the greater

"The dung fuel... blended with water and dried in the sun to produce a circular briquette, is wonderful for heat and preserved embers, much like the Irish peat."

growing season and fertility of the lower valleys) is thus able to afford more elaborate material and labour.

Stone and, latterly, pressed clay bricks constitute the walls in all structures, both being plastered with clay inside and out. Ceilings, floors and the flat roof are constructed by laying, firstly large and then perpendicular layers of successively smaller timbers. When this mesh is sufficient, damp loose clay is tamped into it to considerable thickness until a solid level upper floor is founded. Abodes are of two or three stories, with animals wintering on the ground floor. Cooking, sleeping and other living rooms are found on the other floors. The flat roofs don't have much precipitation to cope with, and provide an excellent work space. Sometimes there will be a penthouse built at one corner of the roof. This may house a shrine, and act as study and retreat. The lack of moisture, and consequent absence of moulds and fungus, permits the external exposure of joist ends protruding through the wall, and indeed the houses seem to need little in the way of maintenance once they are well founded the first day. Whitewash, which seemed to be of a white mineral clay base, more barite than lime, is used but not universally, generally only in certain places or aspects. Lucky or sacred symbols may be found alfresco, such as a painted red triangle brightening an otherwise blank and windowless wall. Inside, furniture is minimal and essential, with space and lack of clutter defining the Zanskari household. One sits upon a fleece or felted mat at the low Tibetan table. You produce your own delft for the meal from within your sleeve. Food and drink preparation requires the roasting pan, the boiling pot,

"Shelter is strong, sensible, and usually quite spacious..."

the kettle (all copper to bronze, as these offer the most efficient conversion of the scarce fire for cooking purposes), and the churns. The twig and dung fire appears on the floor. To sleep, one unrolls the fleece and covers oneself with layers of woollen blankets. Windows may be large or small, but rarely glazed (glass must be carried in over the mountains), so they are sealed in winter with plastered-up temporary clay bricks. While open in the summer months they invariably provide wonderful vistas.

Two rooms in the house are dedicated to defecation, one on a second story, with a hole in the middle of the floor for dispensing, and a sealed ground-level room for receiving and storing the wastes. In the spring, the lower cell is unsealed and cleaned out. The precious and nutritious humus is the source of their topsoil and its fertility, hence it is carefully managed and applied to the fields.

Building itself is carried out by both sexes. I saw women mixing clay and water like cement, working with a fellow laying the clay blocks. All in all, divisions of labour roles are less distinct to European eyes [*times have thankfully changed in western society since I wrote this*], with either men or women preparing food, minding infants and tending to other domestics. There are exceptions. Men tend to spin, though men and women both weave. Men plough, women weed. Men tend remote grazing herds and travel to trade; women largely remain close to habitation.

The Lamas are drawn to the heights for their abodes, and they are structures to behold! A few hundred apartments glued to the nearly vertical face, enduring for many centuries without benefit of slide-rule, computer or "trained engineer" in sight. They don't happen all at once. It is for succeeding generations

to add, or retrofit, extensions and afterthoughts to meet archi-
tectural needs as they arise (refer to photographs and account
of Fuktal Lamasery in Chapter 16). This is the wonder of innate common sense, of *seeing* loads and stresses and requirements for support to endure in time. The structure-in-progress
stands for anyone to view at any point as resembling so much
as a pure organic growth. Bricks and mortar for the sacred
constructions share the secular constituent, but how can one
even utter this?

FAMILY

Marriage, and family structure, is adapted to the finite capacity
of the landscape to support human life. Polyandry is the practice, often taking the form of a woman marrying two or more
brothers, though the husbands may be unrelated. This reduces
the potential number of offspring arising from a given community, and has resulted in a static and supportable population.
Hence the union of two (or more) men with a woman produces
a family. There are indications of high infant mortality; surviving childhood, however, gives a reasonable chance of living a
long life. Say the marriage produces four surviving children,
two boys and two girls. One son becomes a Lama; the other
is joined in a polyandrous marriage in tandem with another
young man. One daughter becomes a nun; the other marries
two brothers from a distant village. Zero population growth!
Divorce is an uncomplicated business and yours alone. It requires simply a "Goodbye" and another place to go. But let us
not skip ahead, as the nuptials, like anywhere, are the vehicle
for much custom, rite and general community excitement.
If the girl is coming to the men's home, the grooms' friends
travel by yak and horseback, sometimes over a hundred miles

Fantastic hats of woven split cane are
worn during wedding journeys

of mountain path to fetch her. This visit occasions a pageant
which in a playful way is reminiscent of the time when a bride
was taken by force (over a thousand years ago). Typically, a
dozen or more men, resplendent in their silver and brilliantly
dyed woollens, ride their horses and yaks to the bride's village,
leaving the groom(s) waiting at home. They are offered every
hospitality, including a surfeit of *chang* and some rare rice
(carried in from India). They partake of all, but all the while, as
the custom has it, complaining to the bride's family and mocking every offering. The bride finally appears, and she is heaped
with scorn and ridicule. Music, dancing and more *chang* follow, when suddenly they mount their horses and gallop away,
the bride in her white up behind one of the men. Stopping at
each *chorten* or holy place along the way, the oboes and drums
appear, and the dancers sway. This continues until they reach
their destination, whether it is an hour's or a week's distance,

where they are met with equal rigour by the grooms' village, before concluding the final rites.

RELIGION/EDUCATION

Religion is based on our impulse to divine and perhaps geometricise the universe and the relationships of all within, and to attain a sustaining faith which will enable us to cope with those events which dwell beyond our comprehension. It provides a caption for our experience, a navigable course. Referring a puzzle to the delineation of an astrological chart or to the relevant apostle by way of suppliant petition are equal expressions of this urge. The answers may be impositions upon reality. But they are very useful, and the source of much comfort. They provoke communion with each other and the beyond.

Hypothesis: Where one religion supersedes another:

1. The existing religion, in the natural course of events, must have become a top-heavy institution, implying conflict, corruption and other abuses which have impinged upon the purer requirements of subscribers;

2. The successor possesses a fresh face for the intellectual and emotional interpretive, but content (considerations of ritual, habit, morality, numerology, etc) does not differ significantly;

3. It must seamlessly adapt to the sacredness of local loric place, and;

4. It must produce a plausible calendar.

In Tibet there was a religious transformation circa the eighth century (which curiously and chronologically parallels St. Patrick bringing Christianity to Ireland, displacing or at

least profoundly altering the Celtic Druidism). Padmasambhava brought Buddhism to Bon Tibet (from the subcontinent).
Now, I am even less a Bon scholar than I am a Buddhist scholar, but Bon seems to me quite graphically as being a wild em-
brace of stark reality, and this is how the simple directness of
Buddhism was able to take hold in Tibetan hearts. The "weaving of Jo-Jo Druguma" (the Bon creation myth) encompassed
the new god. The immigrant Buddhism made the existing hab-
its, deities and feast calendar its own, which is what, of course,
distinguishes Tibetan Buddhism from Buddhism. The central
tenets remained the same; the cultivation of compassion within a world conditioned by desire and suffering. The "simple directness" means that Buddhism appealed to the spirit of place
here, which needs must shine through the vision and the practice of whatever religion would be embraced by the denizens of
this landscape.

A child of Zanskar awakens into a frank world. Heaven is
the serenity on the Buddha's lips. Hell is a collection of insidi-
ous Bon masks. All in all they constitute a pantheon, a portrait
gallery of psychological types, residual in each of us, which are
presented for the wider, collective edification. These players
portray graphic sex and death, masks of passion, reminders
of mortality, being the holographic actors upon a chimerical
stage. Nihilism has been consequently ascribed to Tibetan
Buddhism, but this misses the point. To grow up in a world of
constant, conscious reminders of elemental causes and moti-
vations imparts an uncluttered immediacy of experience. Here
one must duck under a prominent erect phallus upon entering
the alcove of a holy *gompa*. It is there to remind you of where
you are coming from. *Our* "sacred" and "profane" blend considerably into each other and this engenders a self-sufficient,

matter-of-fact outlook, with less opportunity for hang-ups and confused mental states. And very little interest in judging any-one else's behaviour. It all makes for a different world, which must be instanced:

- Stealing, as we call it, is common here, perhaps even more so in Lamaseries, where elaborate timber locks on quarters are the order. But, confronted, the "thief" has no qualms; "Did you take my amulet, Norbay?" "Yes," says Norbay, produc-ing it from within his inner sleeve and handing it back with a smile. *Guilt as an element in human psychology does not occupy anywhere near as similar an importance as it does in our world, and this represents a refreshing departure in terms of motivation.*

- In our society, a common response to extreme eccentric pubescent or adolescent behaviour is to "treat" it by chemi-cal, mechanical or psychological means. The impulse is then frustrated by the intervention and, in mutation to survive, manifests as inwardly- or outwardly-directed vio-lence. Hence, a vital time of transition and initiation, the zenith in the quest for identity defined as much by "what I am not" as "what I may be", indeed all that is wonderful about the formation of personality, is squelched. Whereas, the dawning of juvenile aberrance in Zanskar is accorded benefic space. Received as a gift by the community, "abnor-mal" behaviour is allowed to run its course without tether. *The untrammelled tendency does not turn anti-social and, if in the rare case it is not resolved by adulthood, merely confirms the presence of a shaman in their midst.*

Hence Tibetan Buddhism struck this untutored observer as being chiefly concerned with attaining an unflinching grasp of reality (both inner and outer, though these boundaries blur), as it is only through the absence of delusion that any spiritual progress may be attained. Lamas and lay-folk alike employ various means to steady the focus in the course of their day-to-days. *"Om mani padme hum"* is constantly on the lips of the devout, whether walking through the mountains or weeding in the fields. The hand-held prayer-wheel is turned, as each revolution propagates blessings. The habit is to circumambulate (walking sun- or clock-wise) around *chortens, gompas,* and other holy sites. Whether lay or Lama, one is on a journey of many lives lived in various worlds, and the focus is fixed to hasten one's arrival at journey's end, which is enlightenment and the absence of the need to return to any of these planes (though a still higher attainment is to choose, post-enlightenment and out of compassion, to return to this world to facilitate others on their way).

In the Lamasery, all of this concern is taken to another octave, though even the various sects hold "the way" in differing regard. The *Gyalugpa* (Yellow Hat sect) would seem to seem to be the conservatives, entertaining a status quo – you study, offer devotions, and stay to the straight and narrow, and eventually, after so many incarnations, enlightenment happens. The "red hats", *Dog-pa*, are perhaps more liberal, allowing marriage and more spontaneity. Whereas the *Kargyupta* sect holds to a direct, here and now approach, which seemingly demands the ultimate attainment right now, in this lifetime. But all share absolute devotion to the Buddha's role-model of cultivating the mind's ability to distinguish between the transitory and the unchanging, for it is this discretion which ultimately leads to liberation and the goal of *nirvana*. In practice, the concern is to occupy the will and the senses along prescribed lines employing *mantra*, *yantra* and *mudra*, or sacred sound, gesture and visualisation, thus rechannelling the senses (which are otherwise the restless source of suffering) towards a creatively conscious goal. "*Om Mani Padme Hum*" represents one such mantra and has been translated:

> *I invoke the path and experience of universality,*
> *so that the jewelline luminosity of my immortal mind*
> *be unfolded in the lotus centres of awakened*
> *consciousness, and I be wafted by the ecstasy of*
> *breaking through all bonds and horizons.*

This presents an opportunity to focus thought, and the power of the language of thought to define reality. The *mantra*, in its poetry, beauty and simplicity, absorbs and directs the mind towards a cultured end. *Yantra* is the contemplation of say, a *mandala* and its geometric order, filling the field of vision with a pleasing, orderly and redeeming aesthetic. *Mudra* is the consideration of posture and gesture, enabling the precept to remain attentive while giving the hands something meaningful to do. The burning of incense occupies the sense of smell, its fragrant and undeniable pungency seemingly able to relieve one of hunger in any sense. Finally, the interludes of cymbal, horn and drum complete the sensual preoccupation, with sound waves occupying a place of extraordinary sacredness due to their ability to even alter matter through which they propagate. As the music (and chanting) accompanying the planting of grain assists it in germination, so the pure sonority of the ringing cymbals prepares the novitiate for the truth (*dharma*). Taken together, these considerations preoccupy the mind of the practitioner, and increase the chances of some spiritual progress occurring.

Day-to-day life in the *gompa* is something more and something less than this, however. Before dawn, twinned, deep-throated Tibetan horns (the *dun-chen*) sound the summons to *Puja* (devotions) from high upon the balcony of the main temple. Sixty monks and Lamas, Paddy and I, and several dogs assemble inside. There is no false piety or externally imposed discipline here. Between cups of salted buttered tea and *tsampa*, the elders carry out hour-long chants from the *Prajnaparamita Sutras*, consecrating the same whole grain which younger and more restless monks are flinging at each other across the aisles. The incense burns, the enormous plaster Buddha looks on serenely, and each is left to his own spiritual capacity.

Some young boys of monks catch my eye. In their distraction and boredom they are moulding each their own mini-Buddhas out of barley flour and butter; surreptitiously, would I be willing to judge the best one from amongst their efforts? The deepest gong sounds as I accept and, one by one, the lads' sculptural efforts are somewhat subtly passed to me as I see I am coming under the gaze of the high Lama, who sees all and just smiles. The sculptures are well-fashioned, and difficult to choose between, and I must pass them quickly hand-to-hand to keep them from melting and losing their form, but a winner emerges which I announce *sotto-voce*, further indicated by a discretely extended pinkie in the direction of the victor followed by an upwardly-turned thumb. Hence I contribute both jubilation and disappointment in the resounding midst of neither.

158

Matriculation from one grade of Lama to another depends upon certain set tasks. At some point, one progresses no further without the experience of three years, three months, and three days in solitary meditation, generally in a sealed suite into which food and drink is passed, though one must fall back upon one's own light. Returning to the fold, the "spiritual debates" warrant mention. These are formal gatherings of the brotherhood during which the would-be adept demonstrates not only his grasp of scriptural doctrine, but also his own wit (personality) and spontaneous ability to flesh out his practice under intense and learned scrutiny. These presidia present opportunity to give voice to understanding, with the resulting intellectual interaction providing fodder, both for the novitiates in the audience to ruminate, and for those on high to pronounce clear assessment upon.

Apart from their ritual and devotional activities, Lamas perform many other functions as well. *Gompa* (Lamaseries) are the source of the Mandalic Art of Tibet, the woodblock printing of books and moreover the manufacture of paper. Lamas attend and bless the sowing of grain. They construct the long Mani walls and carve the sacred characters into the stones. They build geometric statuary known as *chorten* (or *stupa* in India), which represent the five constituent elements of earth, water, fire, air and ether (again, the reinforcement of barebones reality for the passers-by), and act as repositories for old books or the bones of saints. Indigenous spirituality restricts industrialisation. Utilitarian employment of the wheel is taboo. I did not find so much as a wheel-barrow, let alone a cart for a horse in all of Zanskar. Rotary movement is considered far too sacred to be sullied by concerns of getting a job done quicker or easier. It was a conscious rejection of technology, consistent with the priority of focussing upon the spiritual, and making do with the material. (Yes, grindstones mill the barley, and at the Karsha *gompa* I saw that clever water-driven incense grinder. But otherwise, natural motion, in the form of wind or water, is reserved to whip flags and other engines of prayer). Major *gompas* have their lines of fixed prayer wheels, which the circumambulator twirls as, chanting, he passes. This is deemed the most appropriate use of circular technology, apart from the creation of the annular calendar.

MEDICINE

I had no recourse to medicinal needs during our time in Zanskar, though I did seek out traditional Tibetan practitioners in the course of a subsequent contemplative and pastoral visit to H.H. the Dalai Lama's retreat in Dharamsala. There I was ministered by His Holiness's astrologer-cum-doctor who, having scribed my astrological chart and gazed at me during a two-hour long consultation, prescribed diminutive black balls of concentrated (and blessed) herbs. My impression of these was that they were extremely potent and catalytic, promoting out-of-body sensations followed by severe purgative action. That I did not feel entirely well after this course brought on the response, not unlike homeopathy, of "Feeling worse? That's a good sign!", and I did not protest. Our time in Zanskar was not sufficient to mine much in detail – we did not have Margaret Meade's thirty years – though I did wonder about the apparent lack of a socialist approach to medicine and that many may well be falling through whatever net that may exist. But this is all beyond my competence.

ART

The art of Zanskar is restricted to the mediaeval and religious. It was not for the lay people to produce impressionistic and fanciful flights, performance pieces or bravura sculpture, but for the Lama to produce the imagery and calligraphy which, again, will sharpen the focus upon the ultimate goal (*bod*=light). And this is exquisite: the *Mandalic* art, of pleasing geometry, an octagon of composition circling a ninth, and central theme; sculptures of the Buddha from palm-sized up to gargantuan proportion; fresco wheel-of-life (*sheepay-corlu*, as they have it, a recurring and dominant theme), lovingly tendered upon shaded walls under graceful colonnades; the exquisite calligraphic carvings of short verses upon stones for placement in *mani* walls. Finally, the sand paintings, laboured and hunched over for days, producing absolute transcendental images, only to be destroyed and cast to the winds after some hours of exhibition, to reinforce the passing nature of it all.

CRAFT, METALLURGY AND JEWELRY

Art and craft both share "skill" and "cunning" as terms of definition in my Oxford and, though they may dispute their boundaries, craft, before art, is firstly necessity-driven, yet not without its ornamental moments. The plough is carved from apricot wood with care, its mole-board of delicate curve; the purpose is to turn the sod, but what sumptuous and justified grace achieves this end? The tracery and halters linking plough to beast may be described with infinite sensibility in pleasing leatherwork, yet no thing to defeat, nay, but to reinforce the ultimate function. Furniture may be rough-hewn, but every mortise and fixing peg whispers the presence of an artistic and visionary validity beyond measure.

There is a very fine sense of smelting and casting. It is claimed that the small, paired hand cymbals are cast from a seemingly impossible alloy of "the five metals", gold, silver, copper, tin and iron. Indeed, all of the musical instruments, from gongs and larger cymbals through to drums and intricate oboes are fabricated with infinite precision. Equally, one need only gaze upon a common teapot to see the genius of the coppersmith, and this excellence extends to the various other cooking vessels.

The jewellery may be a bit crude at times, with stones (turquoise, lapis, garnet, amber, coral, etc.) appearing as-they-are-found (uncut and unpolished) and set into a rough and approximate silver filigree, but I found all of this more to my own tastes than most European jewellery. Castes as such do not exist in Zanskar, yet (strangely) my informants suggested that those who worked with gold were of a lesser order.

Music

The Tibetan for "music" is "*damal-soonan tung*" (literally, "drum-flute libation"). There is a fine array of orchestral instruments to summon every mood and emotion. The *dunchen* is a low-noted horn of over seven feet in length, in effect a straightened tuba, generally played in pairs in long, single deep notes to set up the highly-prized quaver betwixt them. *Hareep* is the onomatopoeic reeded oboe which, unrestrained, soars up and plummets down its scale in absolute abandon. Flutes (*soonan*) are rarer, played solo with contemplative, slower notes like a Japanese *shaku-hachi*. A wide range of cymbals are driven on by *damal* of various sizes, from the tabla-sized session drum to a larger timpani-like fixed drum in the *gompa*.

The music produced falls into one of two major modes. The liturgical, often accompanied by chant, proceeds with saturnine gravity over an hour or more to slowly build to cacophonous resolution. The secular and popular, dominated by oboe and drums, involves free-form, wild and ecstatic improvisational pieces which I could imagine John Coltrane, Herbie Hancock or Miles Davis sitting in with quite comfortably.

THEATRE

Theatre, like the visual arts, is not open to innovation, but relies upon fixed repertoire to work through a seasonal round of dramas, which are Bon in origin but with the necessary Buddhist nuance. Actors are drawn from the ranks of Lamas, the scale of the production reflecting the size and wherewithal of a given Lamasery. Set to rollicking music, these set piece morality plays largely concern themselves with the human condition, confronting the audience with existential dilemmas, a sprinkling of humour sugaring the dire and hopeless drawing of mortal conclusion.

DANCE

The only evidence of improvisation was found in the movements of the Lama-players, woven into their cosmic dramas to the wailing of the full orchestral ensemble. Otherwise, the secular lay dances (apart from the quite drunken steps of the wedding party merry-makers) are set in traditional choreography. The latter holds an innate, breathless grace, a slow, purposeful and flowing intent in the face of music which is relentlessly chaotic (see Chapter 10, "South"). It was like a balancing yoga act, a proclamation that one could achieve serenity and poise within the context of a wild, anarchical and unruly environment.

CLOTHING

Everyday clothing is almost exclusively based upon wool, and though the fleece of sheep would predominate in its constitution, goat and yak hair would sometimes be woven into this. I saw two principle types of loom, the one a fixed frame shuttle loom which incorporated a seat for the weaver, the other a temporary affair, which may be set up over a distance of thirty feet or more. The cloth produced is stitched into shirts, trousers, summer over-garments and long winter caftans. Or, the mixed tufts may be pounded and felted to make hats and boots, the boots sporting felt soles of over an inch thick. Finer base materials and cloths, of cottons and silks, are imported over the mountains for the making of women's dresses and ceremonial clothing. Leather was not employed in either clothing or footwear.

DEATH

When death comes, the body is "waked" with readings from a sacred Tibetan Buddhist text, which assuage and spiritually condition what they hold to be the still conscious spirit attending and remaining proximate to the corpse. This completed (and it may take days or weeks depending upon the degree of elaboration), the remains are carried up into the rocky heights, hacked to bits, and left to be borne off by the hungry, winged raptors and scavengers. It represents a practical approach, where there is not the soil to dig a grave nor the fuel for cremation, and further reflects upon the local proclivity to regard the body (along with all phenomena) as transitory and, though sacred, relatively unimportant.

LAW

With regards to civil law, I found no evidence of written codes, but the weight of collective opinion kept transactions within refined mores. Where a dispute arises, the contestants refer their case to an elder (the King acted as such within Padum). Behaviour may be best described as premoral. Peaceful actions and relations advise the average Zanskari (though there are exceptions and this excludes the license which may be taken by shamans). Perhaps the occurrence of serious crime here is best illustrated by the last murder committed in Zanskar. It transpired that the deed had taken place some four hundred years previously, yet when people referred to it (and the topic arose a number of times during our travels), they would express shock and horror as though it had occurred recently.

❀　　❀

Appendix B

A Guide to Basic Communication in Ladakh and Zanskar Regions

The following is a list of vocabulary terms collected while travelling from Kashmir through the Dras Valley, up the Suru River, over Pensi-La into Zanskar, north to the Indus, east to Leh, and passing back through the Zanskar region once more between April and August 1981. It is rendered in my own rough and approximate Romanised phonetic spelling. Where known and applicable, language/dialect origin is noted thus:

(T): Tibetan (bpopa) (U): Urdu (K): Kargili (H): Hindi
(B): Balti (L): Ladakhi (Z): Zanskari

Time, Space and Greetings

Hello/Good Day: Julay (Z) Tashi Delek (T)
To a Lama: Kushog la
I/Me: Nya
You: Keerung

How are you? Chee ka ba rut? (Z)

What is your name?   Yere mingna che zarbath? (Z)

                      Nyanrang ni ming na chaizer (L)

                      Khye rang gi tshen-la ga-re-re (T)

Where do you live? Nyrung karu zuksat? (Z)

Where are you going? Gar-sha? (Z) Gar-shet? (L)

I am going to Karsha. Nya Karsha chct. (Z)

When? Nam (Z)

Time: Chu-sutt (Z) Gari (T)

What is the time? Chu-sutt samsong? (Z)

It takes three hours: Chu tso sum ba. (Z)

Now: Taksa (Z) Da ta (T)

Later: Sting-la (Z)

Yesterday: Dank (Z)

Today: Deering (Z)

Tomorrow: Toray (Z)

Day after tomorrow: Nangla (Z)

Hour: Kotso (Z)

Day: Nima (Z)

Week: Lok (Z) Idun (L)

Month: Schin (Z,T) Ida (L)

Year: Lo (Z)

Cosmic Period: Kalpa (T)

Calendar: Loto (Z)

Earth: Talba (Z)

Morning: Nyamo

Night: Petuk (Z)

Stars: Skarma (Z) Nam-kha (T)

Sun: Nima (Z)

Moon: Schin (Z) Dawa (Z)

Space (emptiness, hollowness): Tong-ba (Z) Mal (Z)

Old: Neemnya-pa

New: So-ma

Yes: Yo-re (T) Go (Z) Una (B)

No: ma-go (Z) met (L) min (B)

Here: eeru, eekar, yuru (Z)

There: aru, akar (Z)

Understand: hagua (Z)

Thank you:

       tu-je-che (T,L)

       shabashek (Z)

       menerbani (B,H)

I am learning the language. Nya scot labpit. (Z)

Please teach: Lapches zo

I have ____: Nya ____ yut

May I sit down? Inny doo? (L)

Spring: ston (Z)

Summer: yar (Z)

Autumn: speet (Z)

Winter: gun (Z)

Light: ot (Z)

Sun/Sunday: Nima (Z,L,T)

Moon/Monday: Dawa

Mars/Tuesday: Mingmar

Venus/Wednesday: Lakpa

Jupiter/Thursday: Purbu

Mercury/Friday: Raksang

Saturn/Saturday: Spinba

WEATHER, TRAVELLING, FOOD, DRINK, SHELTER AND MARKETING

Today is sunny: Deering nima gala-duk (Z)

Will it snow today?: Deering kha yung rak? (Z)

Snow: gang (T) kha (Z)

Rain: charpa (Z)

Cloud: schrin (Z)

There is a surfeit of wind: Lungs-po monpo (Z)

The streams flow when the sun shines: "Nima gyalyung tokpo chunmo-duk". (Z)

Stream: tokpo (Z,L)

River: sansk-po (Z,L)

Bridge: zamba (Z,L)

Boat: tu (Z,L)

Walk: dul (Z)

North: chang (L,Z)

South: lo (L,Z)

East: shar (L,Z)

West: nup (L,Z)

Drink: co-re (Z)

Tired: nal derak (Z)

How many kilometres? Kilometres tsa mi-ek? (Z)

"I do not know": "Gyus met" (Z)

Sleep: deeka (Z)

Eat: kharji

Food: conna (H,B) kuru (Z) nyiti (L)

Carry: por-shay (Z)

Home: kung-pa (Z)

Price: rinn (Z)

Room: nangla (Z)

Cold: drang-mo (T) trung-mo (Z)

Warm: stante (Z)

Tea: cha (T,L,Z)

Drink tea: cha tung (T,L,Z)

Water: chu (T,L,Z)

Salt: tsa (Z)

Peas: sha-ma (Z) Pod: kow-oo (Z)

Milk: oma (L,Z)

Butter: mar (L,Z)

Skimmed milk: tara (L,Z)

Yogurt: jzo (L,Z)

Cheese: chura (L,Z)

Yak's first milk: tri

Meat: sha (L,Z)

Roasted barley meal: tsampa (L,Z)

Wheat: toe (Z) atta (B) bhakpang (L)

Rice: das (L,Z)

Potato: ahrloo (Z)

Egg: go-nya (L,Z)

Vegetable: tsal, tsol-ma (Z)

Wild Greens: kumuk (Z)

Noodles/Noodle Soup: thugpa (Z)

Flour used as thickener/roux: schrool (Z)

Chapati: roti (Z) tir (L)

Flat Bread: bag-leb (Z)

Boiled tsampa bread: pbawa

Mulberries: tschatoot (K,U,L,Z)

Beer: chang (L,Z)

Firewood: meay shing-top (Z)

"Cooking on the stove": "meay tung boharey kharzhihull"

Bowl: co-re (Z)

Teapot: tchowul (Z) tawoo (L)

Copper pot: zansk (L,Z) zangs-poo (Z)

Spatula: markan (Z)

Candle: chon-tsay, moom-bati (Z)

Mortar and pestle: seck (Z)

"This is for you": "Nyrung nay pia in"

Pen: nyo (Z)

Paper: shugo (L) shugul (Z) druk-shok (T)

Writing: nak-sa (Z) nya-jas (L)

Poet: sumpapo (Z)

Boiling water: chu culches (L,Z)

Road/path: lam (L,Z)

Where does this path lead? E lam caru laybanok? (Z)

"I come from Zanskar": "Nya yos Zanskar" (Z)

Do you have _____?

Nyrungni laga _____ yuda? (Z)

Boot: trad-pa (Z)

Felted Boot: Ba-poo

Socks: han-shoop (Z)

Sweater: pu-tu (Z)

Trousers: hant-se (Z)

Needle: cop (Z)

Thread: hupa (Z)

Knife: cha-bri (Z)

More: tdarung, mon-po (Z)

Less: nutsay (Z)

Up: thalay (Z)

Down: yolay (Z)

Near: nemo

"How much?": "Tsam shik?" (Z)

Carpet: su-den (Z)

Door: ogho (Z)

Window: garhung (Z)

Broom: olmo

Table: mes (Z)

Low Tibetan Table: jhoksay (T)

Before: munglay (Z)

After: stinglay (Z) stingnee (L)

Soap: saboon

Hair: goos-poo (Z) schra (L)

Hand: lakpa

AGRICULTURE & WILDLIFE

Farmer: zamindar (Z,L)

Cow: yak, tsoma, demoo, dzomo (T,L,Z)

Donkey: boom-poo (Z)

Horse: stal (Z) sta (L) tha (B)

Fast Horse: redun, sik-sik (Z)

Slow Horse: yurga (Z)

Sheep: ra-ma (Z)

Hen: jchamo (Z,L)

Egg: go-nya

Grass: stwa (Z)

Straw: sa (Z)

Barley: nas (Z)

Seed: sowen

Flower: min duk

Rope: tak-pa (Z)

Mountain pasture: duk-sar (Z)

Plough: dukchas (Z) tsmochas (U) shol (L)

Mill: rantok (K,B,U) samba (Z)

Wool: geert-pee (Z)

Finished respun wool: yok sheen (Z)

Small yarn spinner: yok-tow (Z)

Earth: talba

Mountain: rhee

Tree: jhong-ma

Bear: dran-moo

Fox: watsay

Wolf: shan-ku

Cat: pay-see

Dog: kee

Dragon: dook

Bee: re-mu (Z) ma-cher (U)

Honey: ran-see

Bird: jee-pa

Eagle: lok

Fish: snya

Children: tu-gu

Husband: na-pa

Wife: annay

Flower: me-duk

Beard: sam-dal

Wood: shing

Carpenter: shing annay

Fire: meay

Smoke: dut-pa

Head: go

Ear: nam-chok

Eye: mik, shan

Nose: snya

Heart: nying

Thumb: tha-po

1st finger: zu-gu

2nd finger: gun-mo

3rd finger: shrin-lok

4th finger: teju-chung

Thigh: lasha

Knee: pigs-mu

Foot: kon-ku

Teeth: so

Tongue: tchay

Fart: trok frio

ADJECTIVES & GENERAL MISCELLANY

Good: gala (Z)

Bad: tsok-po

True: dang-po

Beautiful: de-moo

Old: neemg-pa

New: so-ma

Happy: tat-po

Difficult: gaks-po

Change: spos, spocha

Same: tsuks

Joy: gam-mo

Slow: kulay

Fast: jhoks-pa

Large: chen-mo

Small: chutsay, eetabeetapik

Crazy: shaypatchen

Warm: stante

Cold: trungs-po

Much/many: mon-po

Enough (stop): dik, monposom

Better: sogar galay

Worse: sogar tsokpo

Clean: songma

Dirty: tsok-po

Open : pes/pecha

Close: chuk

Remember: ee-tup

Think: som-ba

Feel: semos

Look: zigs

See: stot

Standing: longsar

Laying: loga

Like: tuttet, tet

He/her: ko

I/me: nya, nay, najas

You: kyrang, nyrung

People: mi

We: mi nyi, mi sum (2, 3)

Boy: nono

Girl: chocho

Child: sonsay, to-go

Brother: acho

Sister: achaylay

Mother: amalay

Father abbalay

Woman: pomo

Male friend: zowoo

Female friend: zamoo

Family: nangsang

Who: su
What: shay
When: nam
Why: choy
How: kazukla
Is; rok, in, bo
To: la
Long: ring-mo
Short: tungsay
Right: tung-po
Wrong: ma-tung
And: tang
More: yang
Yours: kyrung
Mine: nay
Without: kun
This: e
That: tay
Went: song-pin
With nyam-po
From: yos
For: nay pia
Carpenter: shing-kan
Jeweler: sergar
Ring: serdoop
Silver: mul
Turquoise: hew
Valley: long-ba
Climb: staks-pa
Marriage: boxten

Religious, Cultural, & Intellectual Terms

Wheel of Life: kilkor, shepay corlo

Buddhist Yellow Hat Sect : gyalugpa

Red Hat Sect: dog-pa

Direct Path Sect: Kargyupta

"Old Sect": ning mapa

Dukar: Avolokitesvara

Life: tsay

Birth: tschaytay

Death: tschitay

Five constituent elements:

  earth; sa

  water: chu

  fire: meay

  air: lung

  ether: nam

Incense: fway

Book: spe-cha

Tibetan (wooden-covered) book: shos puti

Read: stilches

School: lobtokang

Swastika: yundum

World: jikstom

Knowledge: gyu

Bow: da

Arrow: yu

Sacrificial sword: kalsil

Ceremonial scarf: ka-ta

Prayer flag: dar-shok

Great copper horns: dunchen

Oboe: har-eep

Flute: soonan

Drum: dhamal/dhamen (Z,L), pak-chen (Z)

Music: dhamal soonan tung

Dance: semcha tung

Astrologer: la-pa

King: gyalpo (T,L,Z) raja (H,B,U,T,L,Z)

NUMEROLOGY

1: chig

2: nyi

3: sum

4: shi

5: nya

6: drug

7: dun

8: gya

9: gu

10: chu

11: chu-chig, etc.

20: nyi-chu

21: nyi-chu tsa chig, etc.

30: sum-chu

31: sum-chu so chig, etc.

40: shi chu

41: shi chu she chig, etc.

50: nya chu

51: nya chu nya chig, etc.

60: drug chu

61: drug chu re chig, etc.

70: dun chu

71: dun chu don chig, etc.

80: gya chu

81: gya chu gya chig, etc.

90: gu chu

91: gu chu go chig, etc.

100: tham-pa

1,000: tog trag chig

10,000: tri chig

100,000: bum chig

COLOURS & MINERALS

Colour: see

White: kaiul Z,karpoo(L)

Yellow: serpoo

Gold: sercha

Orange: merpo

Red: marka

Light green: nyoka

Dark green: zangku

Brown: mucha

Purple: muckpo

Light blue: nyonpo

Dark blue: nakpo

Black: nak-ka

Amber: shor-lo

Silver: mul

Turquoise: hew

Copper: zansk

Appendix C

Sayings and Witticisms from Zanskar

(Compiled with gracious further assistance from H.H. The Dalai Lama's Librarians)

"The head moves when only one hair is pulled."

"Speech is like froth, experience like beads of gold."

"His tongue bears witness against his mouth."

"China is spoiled through suspicion; Tibet through hope."

"The time to make men with clay."

"Men like flatterers, and dogs follow those with dysentery."

"To circumambulate while walking."

"Like the weaving of Jo-Jo Druguma."

"The home where blood from my navel was spilt."

"If the rope snaps, the load will be light."

"All that one hears is not speech; all that one sees is not food."

"He possesses only three ideas."

"To snap a twig in the face of a man."

"Spring days grow longer and longer; Mother's bread smaller and smaller."

"Scriptural advice to an ass."

"He looked for the donkey on which he was mounted."

"Without disturbing the bird or the egg."

"If three men are agreed, the Abbot's goat becomes a dog."

"Though the dzomo wanders to Chang Tang, still the tether remains in the lad's hand."

"He who ploughs after consulting his yak."

"Even if the honest meet death, they never abandon their nature."

"If the upper millstone is not heavy, the lower moves."

"An old devil is better than a new god."

APPENDIX D

ANCILLARY FIELD MAP

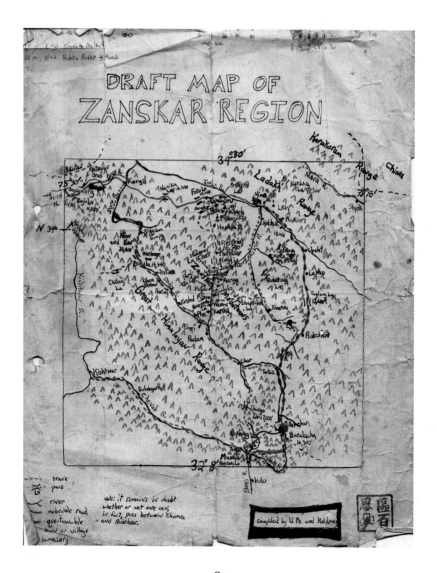